THE LAUGHTER OF PROVIDENCE

Stories from
A Life on the Margins

HAROLD TURNER

The
DeepSight
Trust

A New Zealand Initiative for Religion and Cultures

ISBN 0-9582012-4-2
First published 2001
The DeepSight Trust
PO Box 87-362, Meadowbank
Auckland 1130, New Zealand.
www.deepsight.org

Typeset in Times New Roman and Frutiger.
Design and artwork by Streamline Creative Ltd, Auckland.
Cover design by Sypko Bosch.

Printed through Colorcraft Ltd. Hong Kong

Contents

Preface   7

INTRODUCTION   9
Religious persecution in Western societies. How I see my stories.
The laughter of Providence. Background: home and school.
University: from engineering to the ministry. From Dunedin to London
and West Africa.

STORY ONE: MORAL RE-ARMAMENT   19
My new Gospel confronts the Oxford groups. A critic converted.
Moral Rearmament: Switzerland and Edinburgh. In and out and in again;
MRA 'down under'. In Britain and West Africa. How I see MRA now.
A historic movement, but a new cultural situation.

STORY TWO: INDIGENOUS CHURCHES: AFRICAN AND MAORI   30
The man on the beach: a casual encounter changes my life. What was it?
An all-African church? The man in the next room: meeting the Mennonites.
Can a church include polygamy? A continent interacts with Christianity.
Healing of body and mind. Basic cultural changes. The tribals' worldwide
movements. Persecuting the powerless. A new place in history.
What they can teach us.

STORY THREE: THE RASTAFARI   48
Jamaican slavery. Ras Tafari the Ethiopian deliverer.
Rastafari in Birmingham. Rastafari in New Zealand. Maori Rastafari

Contents

in prison. 'Kidnapping a policeman'. A leader in prison. Christopher Campbell's killing. Repercussions. Suppression of the records. Who are the Rastafari?

STORY FOUR: THE 'MOONIES' OR THE UNIFICATION CHURCH   67
The 'Third Adam' from Korea. The horror stories. Encounter at the front door. Developing friendships. Dangerous friends. The controversial conferences. A financial mystery. Unificationists in New Zealand. Defending the Moonies. International 'front' organizations. Married by Moon. A changing story.

STORY FIVE: RELIGIOUS PERSECUTION IN BRITAIN   84
The great century of religious persecution. Petty official discrimination. 'Ban the Moonies'. Scottish Church uncertainties. Television slaughter. The Daily Mail libel. Attacks from the Government. The Attorney-General three-year fiasco. An uncertain victory. Keeping Moon out of Britain.

STORY SIX: EUROPEAN GOVERNMENTS PERSECUTE RELIGION   99
Mormons and MRA in Britain. Scientologists' battles: 12 years in Britain, 20 years in Italy. Hindus, Exclusive Brethren, Unificationists again... 'Getting' Moon on tax evasion. European Parliament joins in. The Cottrell Report. Impractical controls. Human rights and the Enlightenment. Discovering myself on human rights.

STORY SEVEN: THE AFRIKANER CHURCHES IN SOUTH AFRICA   114
Guest of the academic world. From victualling stop to settlers. Broken by colonial conquest. Recovery by apartheid. The Nico Smith story. In and out of the Broederbond. White minister in Black township. Johan Heyns, martyr. In the homes of both parties. Banning and boycotting, or bridge-building. Against the stream in Britain. South Africa rejoins the world.

EIGHT: WHAT THESE STORIES SAY TO US   132
More than autobiography. The common thread: unacknowledged Western persecution. Another personal story. Stories yet to come. Why does secular society bother to harass religion? Christendom: three worldviews on the sacred and the secular. Secular society attempting a philosophy. Two new relations to the sacred. Further implications for the churches. From theology to ideology and back.

Endnotes   150

Index   156

A note on the text

Because the times and locations of the stories in this book range so widely around the world from the early 20th to the early 21st century, the following chronology of the author's whereabouts may prove useful to readers:

1911-1954 New Zealand
1954-1955 London, England
1955-1962 Sierra Leone
1963-1966 Nigeria
1966-1970 Leicester, England
1970-1972 Atlanta, USA
1973-1981 Aberdeen, Scotland
1981-1989 Birmingham, England
1989-   Auckland, New Zealand

Preface

These seven stories are both autobiographical and unplanned, for although I was personally involved with each of the religious groups described, they all came my way unexpectedly or even contrary to my intentions. They are not general studies of the movements concerned, although my personal story would not make sense without some background material.

Together they form a series of case studies on the fragility of religious freedom, and on the readily aroused public hostility to religion in Western secular societies that leads to harassment or even outright persecution. While my stories concern marginal rather than established faiths they provide a warning prognosis for the future, and expose the hypocrisy of much of our proclaimed tolerance and religious pluralism. These are stories about ourselves that no one wants to know.

Each story is self-contained and could be dipped into or read in any order, although stories four to six do have an inter-connection. Likewise those who want only a story could skip the Introduction and the concluding reflections in Chapter 8; but that would be to miss the overall point of the book and of its title. Those who want to explore various features of the stories or the relevant literature a little further will find help in the Endnotes towards the back of the book.

It is impossible to thank all the actors in the stories. Most of them will never know they have made the essential contributions. I can, however, thank once more those associated with me in the DeepSight Trust who have provided the necessary support and production services: John Flett for the probing conversations, Tim Chamberlain and the Streamline Creative Ltd. staff for their production skills, Sypko Bosch for his cover and other design flair. For proof-reading and critique my grandson Joseph, who revealed unsuspected talent. In Story Three Angus Gillies sharing his own knowledge of the East Coast Rastafari made an invaluable contribution towards accuracy.

In retrospect to put this book together seems obvious enough, yet I doubt it would have happened but for the encouragement of my minister, Graham Redding, to tell these stories on successive Sunday evenings in 1994 to our congregation at Somervell Memorial Church, Remuera. It was the warmth of their reception that suggested they deserved this more permanent form.

Harold Turner
Auckland
March 2001

Introduction

First let me give a pointer to the stories I have chosen to relate. When in 1989 Maude and I left Britain to come back to spend the rest of our retirement in New Zealand, there were three parties at the airport to see us off; including some of our own family, of course. The others were not personal friends, nor from the Selly Oak Colleges where I had last worked for eight years, nor from the United Reformed Church of which I was a minister and where we had worshipped in Birmingham. They were from a marginal and somewhat despised Christian denomination – the Seventh Day Adventists, and from one of the so-called 'sects and cults' vehemently rejected by the churches – the 'Moonies', the Korean-founded Unification Church. And to make it worse, while I was quite surprised, I realized later that I could not have wished for anything more satisfying!

In this small event there is mirrored a large section of where life has taken me – among the marginal, the unpopular and rejected, especially among the new and unknown religious movements. Some of their stories are therefore interwoven with mine, and to that extent this book is personal and autobiographical rather than systematic or academic; it is confined to my experiences and reflections.

There have been five of these new movements or communities in which

I have been especially involved. I hope to give some account of each in these successive stories, and I now list them in advance. In addition to the Moonies or Unificationists who were at the airport, there have been the African independent churches, the Rastafari from Jamaica, the Afrikaner churches in South Africa, and the one I shall begin with as the first I encountered back in the 1930s, the Moral Rearmament movement.

Religious persecution in Western societies

New religious movements like some of these appeared in tribal societies soon after the great expansion of European peoples into the rest of the world after the western hemisphere had been opened up by Christopher Columbus; ever since there has been a steady flow of what I call interaction responses to European culture and its Christian faith, with a great proliferation in the 20th century in most continents. It is in this last century that there has been a growing popular and Christian, almost ideological concern for the poor, the oppressed, and the powerless, manifest in 'liberation' theology ('God is the God of the poor'), anti-colonialism, the political demands of indigenous peoples and the guilt complex afflicting Western élites.

It seems that I have been led into a section of the 'poor and oppressed' that has escaped the above concerns – the 15 to 20 million people currently in these new religious movements, especially in the Americas, Africa and Oceania, and including that strange Unification Church out of Korea, the 'Moonies'. Because they have been either misunderstood, unknown and feared, or unpopular and rejected, their story is also a story of modern religious persecution, and my part in their story often concerns their right to recognition and to religious freedom, in a world that proclaims this freedom in theory but so often denies it in practice.

Two of the stories will also tell of the unrecognized persecution of authentically religious bodies by modern states in the Western world, especially where it would be least expected, in Britain and in Continental countries, and by such a modern creation as the European Parliament. Again my stories are not systematic historical accounts, but recollections of where I have been involved and how I have seen it. Western writers and news agencies keep us informed of the religious persecution occurring in the non-Western world, especially by Muslims, but ignore the harassments and outright persecution in the midst of their own societies. It is usually a case of 'us' being horrified by what 'they' do when religions clash in other parts of the world, and turning away from similar things in our midst.

Despite our belief in the great social advances and new freedoms in most of the world in the 20th century as compared with earlier times, there have probably been more religious martyrdoms in this favoured century than in all the previous 1900 years. My stories do not relate to these more extreme and fanatical forms of persecution, which lie mainly in the non-Western world, and which I have mercifully not encountered.

Rather I shall be telling of the less dramatic, more subtle and less recognized forms of attack upon religious movements within Western societies, or by Westerners upon movements in other cultures. This kind of persecution is the more reprehensible in that it occurs in our own societies where human rights are so vigorously asserted, and the public assumption of an increasingly secular society implies that religions are not worth persecuting.

How I see my stories

All of us have ongoing life-stories in which we are the central actors. Each story is of interest to ourselves, and has more of family and public interest than we might think, even when it seems to record a humdrum, conventional existence that could well have been anticipated to run the course it did. But I would be surprised if anyone, looking back, does not identify some unexpected turn in their affairs, for good or for ill, something quite unplanned but with remembered consequences. As someone has put it, 'History is a record of the unexpected more than of the inevitable'.

The extent to which this is true varies greatly from person to person. Some have relatively uneventful lives, nothing that could ever get into the media, and are grateful for the stability and security. Society should be grateful to those who happily accept the unexciting tasks that hold the world together. Others, the restless and the entrepreneurs, live varied and seemingly eventful lives that may be the envy of the 'stay-at-homes', but who in turn admire the latter for faithfully keeping the wheels turning through thick and thin, and upon whom we all depend more than we realize.

Although I admire the former, I seem to belong to the latter without wishing it. In 1951, after 13 years in various new institutions and positions in Dunedin, I accepted a surprise call to be parish minister of the Presbyterian Church in the very small, geographically limited suburb of Opoho. We were happy and established in Dunedin with a holiday 'bach' we'd built at Taieri Mouth, and I went to Opoho with no ambitions for a career that might begin with a few years at Opoho before I sought larger pastures. I said that I must go ready to stay for life. Three years later I found myself bound for Britain with four young children, no money, and no job awaiting me.

The laughter of Providence

Why, and what followed, will appear in the stories I am now to tell. Before I do so, however, I want to explain the personal comments that apply to them all; these reflections are not inherent in each story, but each story prompts in me the same response – that I must have been the subject of much mirth in heaven.

It was my friend of several universities, Professor Andrew Walls, who framed it for me. He had been booked to fly from Britain to the university in Sierra Leone, where we both once taught. The day before leaving he had a serious heart failure that demanded an immediate by-pass operation in the splendid Aberdeen medical system, that saved his life. If the failure had occurred on the plane or in Sierra Leone he would have been dead. The planned visit of course was cancelled. A week or so later, in a letter telling me all this, he commented: "If you want to make God laugh, tell him your plans."

Time and again as I have reflected upon my affairs, Andrew Wall's story has summed matters up. It sums up both the beginning and the end of the short story of my stay at Opoho. When I went there anything like these further stories was quite beyond imagination, much less planning. Each of the following stories represents a quite unexpected, unsought experience that has turned my plans right about, even while heaven, knowing better, smiled at my laboured intentions. Providence, as it were, always had the last laugh.

This strong conviction has followed me through all the events now to be related. I emphasize this because it prevents me from taking any credit for my part in these stories, as a pioneer or entrepreneur, or far-seeing prophet with deep insight into strange movements and their virtues or their futures. When doors have opened, I 'happen' to have been there to stumble blindly through and allow the consequences to unfurl. So these are scarcely my own stories and certainly not my own plans.[1]

Background: home and school

Before launching into the first of these stories, perhaps I should offer a little of my personal background and some of the early small but in the end significant examples of Providence in my affairs. My parents came from pioneering South Island farming families in Ida Valley in Central Otago. Between these two families there were 22 children. From those who survived and married I received 34 uncles and aunts. But by a sudden dramatic drop in fertility the 34 produced only 49 cousins, and I have had only one sister.

I saw little of this extended family, for my parents settled in the North Island, in Napier. In that area my father built sturdy timber-frame houses for 40 years, and achieved a modest prosperity by hard work. We survived one of the three greatest known plagues in history – the 1918 world 'influenza' epidemic that killed over 6000 in New Zealand in a month or so. We lived through the Great Depression of the 1930s in which the family lost most of its savings, and New Zealand's most disastrous earthquake in 1931, with some 270 deaths in Napier and Hastings. At that time I was a student working for funds in the summer vacation as kitchen assistant in the cookhouse of the large Whakatu meat freezing works near Hastings, which collapsed before my eyes while I lay helpless on the violently moving ground.

So I grew up in a builder's workshop. When I wanted a canoe, I made it. In the 1920s I made my own crystal radios and then a valve set. I explored Meccano to its limits. My teenage friend, Alan McLeod, and I reached the summit when we spent three months making the Meccano loom. If you turned the handle (with some knack and effort) a strip of woven material was rolled up on the other side!

Looking back on a very happy boyhood, I find there are several small events that stand out as critical in their long-term consequences. We were living in the small town of Havelock North when I finished primary school, and I would have gone on to what was then the Hastings District High School three miles away, for two years of secondary education. But our family doctor's father had been rector of Otago Boys' High School and he knew about schools. He said No! I must go to Napier Boys' High School for full secondary education at a good school. And so it was that I biked a mile, then by bus three miles to Hastings and then the 12 miles by train to Napier, and finally the mile walk up to the top of the hill where the old school was. And back again – walk, train, bus, bike. I finally travelled 25,000 miles in the boys' school carriage on that train. It was a good school and I'd have been nowhere near a university without it.

But it took other small events to get me to university. I was in my third year in what was still called the 6th form, in a second try for the entrance scholarship that was essential if I were to go on to university. I became browned off and stale. A new headmaster came and I fell foul of him. I wouldn't have secured a scholarship.

My parents had heard of the famous Auckland Grammar School, and at Easter 1929 they sent me off there. The school found me board: indeed, I had a room of my own – a six feet square hut in a backyard in Grafton, lit only by a candle. I soon found something better. Several important things happened in those nine months. I had been well brought up in Presbyterian Sunday school and Bible class but never baptized or confirmed. The Rev. David Herron baptized me before the session of St. David's, Khyber Pass, I became a communicant, and I taught Sunday School.

I reached the summit of my sporting career when mysteriously I became *vice*-captain of the Rugby *Second* Fifteen. I wasn't a sporting type, but I was dead keen as a sergeant in the school cadets. So I was one of three from the school who sat for commissions as 2nd Lieutenants in the Territorial Forces. I failed on the Lewis machine gun test. But I worked hard and secured a university entrance scholarship of £60 a year plus tuition fees for three years; this supplied the greater part of the £100 that I managed to live on during each of my six years as a student during the Depression; I still have the notebooks recording each penny spent.

All these events – browned off at Napier, stimulated at Auckland, committed to the Church, failing one exam and passing the other – played their providential part in what was to come. I was soon glad it didn't include the army. There must have been laughter in heaven at my military enthusiasm.

University: from engineering to the ministry

I was planning to become an electrical engineer and earn big money in places like Indonesia. So the next step was to study engineering at the university in Christchurch; but there was then almost no student residential provision and we knew no one. So to find board we decided to write to one of the Presbyterian congregations there. In the Hastings public library I found the church notices in the Saturday edition of the Christchurch *Press*; but which one to write to? Somehow, and for no conscious reason, the minister's name at St. Paul's Church caught my fancy – W. Bower Black – so I wrote to him.

He met me at the Christchurch railway station and drove me to the lodging he had arranged with a widow in the congregation. A year later he moved away, but in that one year he took me walking with him on the Port Hills above Christchurch on his Mondays off. He took me to the great Bible Class Easter camp of those days. He endured my confused attempts at discussion late at night in his study. And at the end of the year his influence led to a change from engineering to arts en route to training for the ministry, and planning to become a missionary – perhaps still in Indonesia, in my naive mind.

Then the great Alan Watson became minister of St. Paul's Church for my five further years in Christchurch. Through him I was in the middle of the most remarkable group of some dozen younger ministers that the New Zealand Presbyterian Church has ever known. They were responding to the exciting new theological currents in Europe associated with the names of the great Swiss theologians Karl Barth and Emil Brunner; they were rediscovering John Calvin and working on the renewal of preaching, teaching, worship and theology in New Zealand. Alan Watson was also one of the founders of the ecumenical movement here, before he was called to Australia, so I was a kind of Wimbledon ball-boy in the early days of the National Council of Churches, which began largely through inter-church relations in the Christchurch area.

I was now studying philosophy at the University but the very small department at Canterbury had become almost extinct. I must have had the worst training in philosophy from the university anyone has ever had in this country. But Alan Watson was no mean philosopher and on Monday mornings he read the set books of the great German philosopher, Immanuel Kant, with me in the manse study. He and the Christchurch Presbytery were largely responsible for the university abandoning its plan to 'save' philosophy by putting it under psychology! And at one stage he was engaged by the university to teach a philosophy course that I was supposed to have. So he and I went and sat in a university lecture room, one on each side of a table, while he lectured me.

Here it may be noted that a year or so later philosophy was re-established in Christchurch (with pressure from the Presbyterian Church) through the appointment of a young refugee from Austria – the later famous Sir Karl Popper, who died in England in 1994.

The third and most important thing that happened to me at St. Paul's – I married a girl from the choir. I'll not go into that in detail. But if I had not gone to that particular congregation I would probably be an engineer. Even if I had changed vocation to the ministry in another congregation, I would have missed the basic theological and philosophic influences that have served me ever since. And I cannot bear to think of having missed out on that girl in the choir.

John Buchan, the great Scottish novelist and public servant who became Lord Tweedsmuir, has an essay called 'The Casual and the Causal in History'. He traces the profound subsequent effects of trivial things like a statesman catching 'flu at the wrong time, or even of a wart on a queen's nose. Likewise for my irrational fancy for Bower Black's name in those church notices. Such was the casual factor that led to all this, and also therefore to all that has followed on.

From Dunedin to London and West Africa

My student days finished with a first class M.A. in philosophy in 1935, followed by three years' ministry/theological training in Dunedin, with a final term in Edinburgh. Then followed 15 years in various kinds of pastoral ministry in Dunedin – at Knox Church, in the first ecumenical chaplaincy among students, in two new halls of residence, and finally in the small suburban parish of Opoho. That story belongs elsewhere and what little relevance it has to the following chapters will appear as we proceed. I can therefore leap ahead to the major change of 1954.

I had enjoyed some occasional part-time teaching of philosophy in both Canterbury and Otago Universities, and the theological teaching that formed part of my student ministries. Teaching, I felt, was my forté, but there was no opportunity then for theological teaching in New Zealand and I was advised to seek this abroad. So in 1954 we migrated to Britain with the hope of getting into one of the rapidly developing new post-war departments of divinity in colleges of education. Although not a trained teacher, with a B.D. I thought I could manage this. I began as a 'temp', teaching Scripture and arithmetic in a London secondary school. It nearly killed me. But I was restored on Fridays, when I was released to lecture in divinity in Goldsmiths, a College of London University that included the largest teachers' college in England.

Goldsmiths had dabbled in divinity teaching with part-timers like me. Or *not* like me, for my predecessor was described as 'an unfrocked Anglican priest, a known Communist, under investigation by the CID'! His set texts were mostly published by the Rationalist Press Association, debunking Christianity. So I saw a bright future for the development of a somewhat more orthodox and scholarly department of divinity, if I could work into a position there.

They offered me a half-time position for the following year, and I seemed to be on the way in. But Providence had other plans. Since arriving in London I had been applying for any full-time tertiary position that came up anywhere. One of these had been to teach Old Testament in the University College of Sierra Leone. In July 1955 when the person offered the position turned it down, they fell back on me – there was no waiting list for jobs in Sierra Leone, still haunted by its reputation as 'the white man's grave'. I later learned that he was a virtually unfrocked Presbyterian minister, escaping from a divorce after an affair with a young woman who had been killed in a motoring accident when driving with him. I seemed fated to succeed some colourful characters! He was in fact a very much better Old Testament scholar, but when I later heard his history, I felt I was perhaps a better appointment.

So in September 1955 instead of settling in London our family found itself on their first air travel – the six of us flying to Paris and a night in a hotel, then all next day on a big Constellation plane to Dakar in Senegal, West Africa, and a night in a very modern hotel, then on the third day in a small plane to a country I had hardly heard of – Sierra Leone. No night flying, and other people paying for it all! What a contrast from the five weeks in a six-berth cabin coming from New Zealand on borrowed money the year before.

Now I found myself in two new worlds. The African college had been founded in Freetown by the Church Missionary Society in 1827, as Fourah Bay College for higher education in this colony of former slaves from America, founded in the late 18th century – one of its laterite stone churches had 1793 on the foundation stone. In arts, science and theology it had long provided the intelligentsia for the whole of Anglophone West Africa. Since 1876 it had been a most unusual part of the University of Durham (founded

1832!) in England, being added to its six constituent colleges as an affiliated but overseas college, subject to the same syllabuses and working for the same degrees. I had gone to the University of Durham to be interviewed for the position. With political independence sweeping Africa the college was in process of becoming the University of Sierra Leone. I was unexpectedly into university work (almost into two universities), by a very strange route, in a very unusual place.

I was to teach within a small Faculty of Theology headed by an African scholar. Not England, but Africa; not a teachers' but a university college; and not religious studies or divinity, but the Old Testament. As Andrew Walls would have put it, I had been telling God very clearly what my plans were ever since we decided to emigrate to Britain. Not much notice seemed to have been taken; and looking back, how thankful I am that they were ignored. A whole new unplanned world was about to open up for us all, and what it contained will be told in Story Two. But first we must go back to my university days in Christchurch and pick up the first of my stories that begins there – the Oxford Group/Moral Rearmament movement.

Moral Rearmament

Now I must tell something of the first of the new and unpopular religious movements that provide the substance of the stories in this series. In my teen years the church I attended gave me what I now see to be a liberal social-gospel form of Christianity. One of the minister's favourite books was Ralph Waldo Trine's *In Tune With the Infinite*, which for the 1920s sounds a foretaste of current post-modern spirituality. I was high on moral idealism that expressed my adolescent enthusiasms and even made me want to be a missionary, but it was devoid of the great mysteries and depths of the Gospel.

My new Gospel confronts the Oxford Groups

In the 1930s, however, I came under the influence of the theological renewal in Europe through my minister, Alan Watson, and J.M. Bates, my second mentor, and of others in the remarkable group referred to in the Introduction. The historic Creeds were coming to life; theology became an exciting enterprise; the great drama of the Christian Gospel dawned upon us. We had answers instead of idealisms, and I wrote six articles about it all in Young Men's Bible Class national magazine, *Foursquare.*

I was therefore able to argue theologically against a new streamlined evangelistic movement that hit New Zealand about 1933, known as the

Oxford Groups. This was a worldwide evangelistic campaign of life-changing that emerged from the activities of an American Lutheran minister, Frank Buchman (1878-1961). He had been a controversial figure in two student ministries, and after opposition on Princeton University campus in 1926 had been asked to leave. In mid-life, at the annual Keswick evangelical convention in England, he had experienced a profound spiritual renewal, and felt compelled to become reconciled to some of his former trustees by confessing the ill will he had harboured towards them.

During this uncertain career he had been developing an unorthodox evangelistic method based on God's guidance (largely sought in early morning Quiet Times to find His plan for the day and beyond), on mutual support in groups, on the four moral absolutes of absolute honesty, purity, unselfishness and love, and on the confession of sin to one another, to the group as a whole, or even publicly.

He then travelled independently as an evangelist, and won more substantial response in the University of Oxford among the post-World War I generation. Through taking a team of his converts to conferences and 'house parties', sometimes attended by thousands, the movement spread in many countries, including South Africa where it was nicknamed 'The Oxford Groups', a name it accepted. Dramatic stories of changed lives among industrialists and trade unionists, journalists, aristocracy and other unlikely candidates for conversion became common. The movement concentrated on community leaders and influential figures – on the neglected 'up-and-outs'. One of its early books, called *For Sinners Only*, was written by A.J. Russell, a converted Fleet Street journalist.

I first met the movement about 1934 during one university vacation, in the form of a small, immature group meeting in the evenings in a Chinese fruit shop in Hastings, where the family was then living. I persuaded them that what they really needed was solid Bible study and I took them through John's Gospel – so I did! Alan Watson had just done this very effectively in the Student Christian Movement in Christchurch. I was able to turn any challenge back into something more intellectual and less personal.

In the next few years I read about the Groups, mostly critical literature. I remember Alan Watson preaching the longest Presbyterian sermon I have ever heard – 45 minutes – in criticism of the Oxford Group movement. And of course I agreed with him. The Groups were naive in their mechanical view of private guidance on tap from God, in their simplified codified morality, presumptuous in their adoption of moral absolutes and in their claims of changing the world, and as for public confession – that was just vulgar.

One of the Oxford Group's early promoters was the stocky Ivan Menzies, the lead comedian in the J.C. Williamson Opera Company that used to bring Gilbert and Sullivan operas periodically to New Zealand. He had a story of conversion from a loose life on the stage, and used all his histrionic skills; this gave the Groups immense publicity. Some university students in Christchurch joined the movement and tried to convert me. Nothing doing! They were the types who had responded least to the theological renewal in which I was sharing. But all the same I was a little frightened of them.

A critic converted

By this time, 1936, I was in the theological college in Dunedin. At our first annual student retreat the respected minister leading it, J.M. McKenzie, testified to how he had found his feet through the Groups. This began to get under the skin of a few of us. But nothing happened till a year later I came across a book by one of my gurus, the distinguished Swiss theologian Emil Brunner – *The Church and the Oxford Group.* His account of why he had identified with the Groups undermined my theological objections and I became open to what it might do for me. In addition my high-flying theological equipment seemed inadequate for the pastoral work I was now doing in North Dunedin as a part-time student assistant to the Rev. David Herron at Knox Church, who had baptized me as a schoolboy in Auckland.

How the new movement hit many Theological Hall students in 1937 is too complex to tell here. Hubert Ryburn, minister at St. Andrew's Church in Dunedin and later Master of Knox College and Chancellor of Otago University, was among the younger theologians but also became identified with the movement and helped many of us. Likewise Dr. Will Porteous at Knox Church, the lanky medico who had founded our church's mission in India, was a keen 'Grouper'. There were a few other church leaders, but most were negative and some were bitterly opposed.

Suffice it to say that my earlier theological enlightenment was now complemented by a more intimate personal conversion. For instance, the absolute honesty challenge led me to confess that I had cheated in the unpopular annual Bible Knowledge examination, held in the theological college after each long vacation. I had come back late for the exam and was allowed to sit it, and very unprepared, in my own room; the Bible was there at my desk! But then this absolute moral standard caught up on me. The staff had no private offices at the college then, so to make my confession meant going to see the very shy Professor John Collie at his home and telling him the wretched story, and being ready to sit again. But the poor man was more embarrassed than I was and couldn't dispose of the subject fast enough. Presbyterians don't confess their sins to one another! And there was no re-sit.

In my new convictions I even wrote to my former minister, Alan Watson, suggesting he had been mistaken in his condemnations, and should think again. Unfortunately I wrote on another matter to his predecessor, Bower Black, at the same time, and put the letters in the wrong envelopes. Bower Black would have nothing to do with the Groups and he wrote ticking me off no end for writing to a senior minister like that, and broke off relations with me. Thirty years later he came across my address in Britain and wrote picking up the threads again; I replied and we were reconciled before he died.

Moral Rearmament: Switzerland and Edinburgh

Subsequent events included attending a Group conference in Australia and then I was part of quite a large New Zealand delegation to their 1938 international assembly at Interlaken in Switzerland. One was Sybil Williams, who became Secretary of the New Zealand Student Christian Movement; she and I spent some time in Geneva visiting the great W.A. Visser't Hooft, then secretary of the world SCM; but he was very canny about this controversial MRA. At Interlaken the movement adopted its own chosen name of Moral Rearmament, as a more meaningful sign of the movement's moral thrust and to facilitate contact with other races and religions, which it was now actively seeking. Someone thought I ought to have a personal pastoral session with founder Frank Buchman; he 'did me over', but I was not impressed. He queried whether I was sure I ought to be engaged to the girl from the choir. Divine guidance indeed!

During the subsequent three months I had as a student in New [Theological] College, University of Edinburgh I was able to continue participation in Scottish MRA activities, and to discuss the movement with Professor John Baillie, who had been the attraction to New College and with whom I was getting on very well. With Emil Brunner's identification to support me, and the judgment that Baillie himself offered me, that this was 'the only vital Christian movement of our time', I asked him why he also did not identify. I could understand his answer – that he would immediately lose any influence in the affairs of the university and among its faculty. It was not for lack of concern, for he was convener of the Church of Scotland Church and Nation Committee with its annual penetrating reports on public affairs, and (unknown then to me) a member of J.H. Oldham's newly-formed top-level thinkers' group down south, 'The Moot', critiquing our culture. Nor did he lack courage, for just 18 months later he was with the army in France and was one of those in the British forces rescued from the beaches of Dunkirk. But MRA was not a viable option for John Baillie in the Church of Scotland and University of Edinburgh. As I shall relate, over 20 years later I was to test this question again in the same Church and city.

In and out and in again

My identification with MRA continued upon return to New Zealand. I was ordained in 1939 as assistant minister at Knox Church, Dunedin, and preached some pretty 'Groupy' but not uninfluential sermons. Within a few months I was expounding MRA on the regional radio. When an MRA film was shown on the commercial circuit in the city I went in front of the cinema screen each evening, clerical collar and all, and gave a personal introduction to it. Only once was I taken severely to task by a senior minister for some of the things I had been saying about MRA.

I drifted out of active association with MRA in the 1940s, as I had not found what I felt was my role as a theological mediator between the movement and the churches. Then MRA brought one of its stage plays to Dunedin, *The Forgotten Factor*. We were asked to billet one of the stage hands. He turned out to be an Australian, a Rhodes scholar from Victoria, who had won the premier poetry prizes at Oxford and published some splendid poetry.[1] So I looked forward to intellectual discussions in the study while the girl from the choir graciously served coffee at intervals. But Michael Thwaites often left *me* in the study and went and talked to *Maude* while she did the ironing or whatever, and to the *children*. This taught me something I needed to see, about myself, my family and my priorities; and here was an intellectual of some calibre, yet serving merely as a stage hand.

So I picked up with the movement again and got to know some of the alcoholics and others with severe problems who were being helped by MRA in Dunedin. This wasn't surprising since I discovered that the Alcoholics Anonymous movement had been founded in the 1930s by two alcoholics in the USA who had been 'rescued' by the Oxford Groups. They had then condensed and focused the group practices into what became the famous 'Twelve Steps' that have provided a model for the host of 'XYZ Anonymous' mutual-help bodies that have sprung up around the world, usually ignorant of their OG/MRA parentage.

I continued my participation sufficiently on one occasion to go to the length of parking our four young children with friends while my wife and I flew to Auckland to take part in an MRA gathering, a quite emancipatory action for a young mother. In 1952 I gave an apologia for the movement in the inaugural address that opened the Presbyterian theological college each year. In this I pleaded for mutual recognition and closer co-operation between MRA with its public social gospel and striking results on the one hand, and on the other various Christian bodies also concerned with the public sphere – J.H. Oldham and his group in England, Dr George McLeod's Iona Community in Scotland, and the National Council of Churches in New Zealand with the Campaign for Christian Order. I had been deeply involved in the latter and much influenced by both the others. The theological students wrote to show their appreciation of this radically ecumenical approach. On the whole I was less publicly and controversially engaged with MRA, which itself was less in the public eye.

In Britain and West Africa

This continued until we left for Britain in June 1954, seeking teaching work. During my temporary appointment teaching in a secondary school, I began to relate to the British MRA activities and its base in Brown's Hotel, London. I remember taking people to see some of the MRA plays that were in continuous production in the theatre they had bought near Victoria Station – our whole family, and on another occasion a party of my school pupils.

I have already related how we were translated from the English educational system into a fast-developing Africa, wherein I still had structural links to the University of Durham. If, however, I was to continue in university teaching with my very modest degrees, I felt the need of doctoral qualifications. So I planned to do a Ph.D. on the obvious subject for me – Moral Rearmament. I could use the staff privileges I enjoyed within the University of Durham structures. MRA needed interpretation to the Churches, and I had extensive materials and experience acquired over two decades. So I registered and secured a congenial professor as supervisor, but it did not work out. The professor left Durham, and it seems this gently smiling Providence was in fact waiting to lead me again into quite another kind of research, and not, as it turned out, for my planned Ph.D. That will be part of my next story, the African research chapter.

There was no MRA member or movement as far as I knew in West Africa, so our only contact remained through the annual long vacation when we expatriates were sent to Britain while the college was closed for the exceedingly wet season. Here I had earlier tried to establish contact with a theologically-minded member of the movement, the Rev. J.P. Thornton-Duesbury, formerly Principal of Wycliffe Hall, Oxford, and then master of the new college of St. Peter's. But a telephone call from this unknown person from 'the colonies' failed to produce the hoped-for invitation to meet for discussion.

On the first visit back we had bought an old inn as a vacation residence in Steeple Aston, a village just north of Oxford, and I became friendly with Robin Mowat, son of a well-known historian and himself lecturing in history in the Oxford Polytechnic. Robin was a committed MRA member and had published several books combining MRA ideas with those of A.J. Toynbee, the famous historian of civilizations. We were in a historical crisis that demanded a change as far-reaching as that which primitive society had made in stepping up to the first civilized societies 6000 years ago; and this step, like the previous one, could only be taken under the aegis of a religious faith expressed through a creative minority such as MRA. This was heady stuff, but Robin filled it out from his knowledge of history, from his wide experience (in Egypt he had once taught Nasser, the future president), and from the striking stories MRA was producing as itself a creative minority. He was the intellectual in the movement, the person who I had been looking for and our friendship continued for several years.

My participation in the movement itself had now virtually ceased. It retained a controversial if less prominent profile, and had become a regular butt for snide media references. Some members of the British Parliament bitterly opposed it and had tried to have its workers banned from entry to Britain, just as if it was one of the later 'sects and cults' such as the Unification Church that appears in some of my later stories.

About 1960 I was persuaded by a Church of Scotland missionary in Ghana to apply for a lecturing vacancy in the Presbyterian theological college there. I had been doing field research in Ghana during mid-session vacations from Sierra Leone, I liked the larger country and its people, and I felt it was time for an expatriate to move on from Sierra Leone. So when on leave in England I went up to Edinburgh for interview by the Church of Scotland missions committee. James Matheson, a senior member of it, had served a term as minister of Knox Church, Dunedin, after my time in that church but while I was still publicly associated with MRA. I thought I had been getting on well with the interview, but when he gratuitously drew the committee's attention to my association with Moral Rearmament I knew from the silent reaction that there would be no appointment. So I got in first and withdrew my application as soon as I arrived home. Again in Edinburgh, as 22 years before, I had found the Church of Scotland unable to accept MRA.

Another little factor swinging the way one's life goes? One of the jobs I have applied for and later thanked God I didn't get! I can think of half a dozen that I tried to put into the plan of my life; but Providence always knew better.

How I see MRA now

I have never wanted to retract from what happened through MRA and I remain grateful for what it did for me and has done for many others. In the 1990s two of our best friends who were both in MRA with us in Dunedin days, published anonymously a little of their story of some of its influence in their lives. The husband, a Christian minister, had a psychological breakdown during which he left his family and went off out of touch and on his own, doing labouring work, although he always sent money for the family support. The psychiatric specialist strongly advised his wife that he would not get better unless she divorced him! But she stuck to her marriage vows and with immense help from MRA folk reared their four children and waited – waited till the day when he would return. As he did, 13 years later. Then he began work as a storeman in a large firm, took a brave lone moral stand in some union matters, and at his retirement farewell the manager described him as having been 'the conscience of the firm'. They enjoyed a happy retirement, supporting local MRA activities, until his death in his 80s, and one daughter has long worked fulltime for MRA in America.

I think OG/MRA made brilliant use of drama of quite professional standard, plays in a contemporary setting with a positive message written by their own members, such as *The Forgotten Factor* (God, of course, but obliquely introduced). Their songwriters also produced their own collection of easily-sung ditties with a simple, commonsense content, such as:

I've got a wise old horsey, and times I've heard him say
The trouble with the world is the folks that live in it,
They've all learnt to get and they've never learnt to give in it.
You'll never build a world, a decent sort of world,
You'll never build a world that way.

I had no embarrassment in enjoying these plays and singing these songs along with anyone.

Although I have always defended MRA from ignorant or unfair attacks, there have been methods I could not defend. One of these has been inviting some prominent person – a media star, national president, business tycoon, university professor, etc. – to be a guest for even one day at an international conference, say at Caux, and to speak briefly about their version of public affairs in the context of the MRA assembly.

This usually produced a few polite moral platitudes, the guest went on his or her way and had no further connection with the movement, which was barely understood. Then visitors found their remarks highlighted in the movement's literature and publicity – so-and-so (with photograph) 'warmly supports the MRA answer', almost as if now identified with the movement. The person feels trapped and used publicly in a way never anticipated, and the final effect is counter-productive. I saw this happen with Dr. Azikiwe, the founding President of Nigeria.

This has been a common way of relating to the 'up-and-outs', but I believe it represents a certain naivety rather than a cynical public relations exercise.

A historic movement

No movement is perfect, but I believe the Church historians have largely ignored one of the influential and dramatic Christian movements of the 20th century, something that Professor John Baillie had seen by 1938. A full-scale life of Frank Buchman by Garth Lean appeared a few years ago.[2] There one can learn of the unscrupulous opposition MRA received from sections of the Church of England, and from certain politicians, which could almost be called persecution, and the mocking by the media. But how many know the origins of Alcoholics Anonymous and all its imitators?

One also learns of Buchman's little known high-level influence in Europe after World War II. He knew well both Robert Schuman and Konrad Adenauer, both Catholics, who were the outstanding statesmen in the reconciliation between France and Germany. The Schuman Plan for uniting them through a European Coal and Steel Community became reality in 1952, and was the ground-breaker for all the subsequent European Community developments.

There are similar more recent stories of reconciliation in Bougainville and other centres of conflict, such as Cambodia. After World War II, MRA maintained an international conference and training centre at a mountain hotel it bought at Caux in Switzerland, where prominent people of all races and religions pass through its summer conferences. There is a smaller centre near Melbourne and premises in Lower Hutt, New Zealand, and elsewhere around the world. It supports a small cadre of fulltime workers in these centres and in its American headquarters in Washington, D.C. It has also experienced the problem of unity that affects other movements as they age.

MRA has never become popular and has often aroused irritation in the Churches, although most church people now have never heard of it; the media have remained almost uniformly hostile. But in 1992 the retired editor of the Church of Scotland's monthly, *Life and Work*, confessed to a new respect for a movement he had written off in the past; he had now seen it for himself in the East making an important contribution from the West to the post-Communist Soviet Union. And in 1988 a 50th Jubilee service for the adoption of the name MRA at Interlaken was held in Westminster Abbey and attended by Anglican and Catholic bishops and other church dignitaries. It doesn't cost much now to bless it! It was rather different in the heyday of the movement, over 50 years ago.

A new cultural situation

The organization, however, keeps ticking over and individuals are still 'spiritually changed' by MRA, occasionally some unexpected person in a prominent position and with public effect. A few 'identify' and remain to engage in further activities, but most pass on, grateful, but continuing either inside or outside the churches. I don't think it will ever regain the influence it once had, since the whole situation in Western culture has changed with the loss of a common public morality to appeal to, and with the vigorous propagation and public acceptance of postmodern worldviews where all things are relative. One might say it is not *moral* re-armament that is needed in Western societies, but basic '*truth* recovery' in all areas of our culture, including the moral.[3]

For me it was my first experience of a new and controversial religious movement, which came my way unsought, and to which my relationship developed in a way very different from that which I kept planning. At least I came to know it from the inside, which was usually more than the critics knew, and that at heart it was quite orthodox theologically, even if its methods were unusual, and that some of these had remarkable results. It turned out to be a very gentle introduction to some of the other movements that Providence had ahead, all unknown to me. But they are for the further stories.

From African Independent Churches to Maori Movements

Before I told the first of these stories I indicated that when I look back upon the consequences of certain small apparently insignificant events, I find that these have played a part seemingly out of all proportion to their significance at the time. This story is of a casual encounter on a beach that changed both my plans, and the whole course of my life.

The man on the beach: a casual encounter changes my life

In 1957, some 18 months after our arrival in Sierra Leone, our family was swimming at Lundi, the ocean beach near Freetown favoured by expatriates. This was something Africans seldom did, but on the beach there was one African in an unusual white gown, with a few others coming and kneeling before him while he placed an iron rod on their heads and said something over them. In curiosity I rather brashly went and asked him about it, but what he told me meant nothing to me and I thought no more of it.

This African, however, had asked where I worked, and a few days later he sent two of his young men up to our house on the university college campus with an invitation to preach in a special service at what he called his

(Opposite) Adeleke Adejobi, the second primate or head of The Church of the Lord (Aladura), founded in Nigeria, 1930.

'church'. Again in curiosity I accepted; try anything once. So on the day I found this big new concrete-block building a bit out in the bush from our city of Freetown, with some 200 people at worship in their white robes, men on the one side and women and young children on the other; and the four-hour service led by the man from the beach, Adeleke Adejobi, wasn't too long, because it was so interesting.

For one thing, without ever deciding to do so, I found myself dancing solo, but with my shoes off! – for everyone left footwear at the entrance. As an important guest I had been seated beside the altar, and I had also been warned that this was a service where a special offering would be received, so I had arrived prepared. Many different organizations and groups formed up from within the congregation and then each in turn danced and sang their way up the aisle to place their money gifts on the large tin tray which still portrayed that its original purpose had been to advertise Johnnie Walker whisky. Some members came several times in different groups with their West African pennies (large bronze coins with a hole in the centre).

The leader had kindly sent me over a note that I would have my own call. When my turn came to walk down to where the tray lay, with the drums going and the full-throated singing, I just could not avoid an amateur imitation of what everyone else was doing, and I broke into some kind of jigging dance, full Presbyterian liturgical vestments and all – in flat contradiction of the Presbyterian tradition of doing everything soberly, 'decently and in order'. I am sure Heaven enjoyed the scene. Apparently the congregation did, for some years later, when working through the records of the church, I came across a report of this service, where 'This European humbled himself, to take off his shoes and dance with us'. That such a minor accommodation to the local situation should have made this impression speaks volumes about the colonial situation.

Much of the service was familiar: the structure of hymns and prayers, Bible readings and sermon, the Apostles' Creed; but much was strange: the possession by the Spirit while prophesying or speaking in tongues or rolling on the floor, the dancing and drumming, the sprinkling with holy water, and the sheer dynamism of these worshippers.

What was it? An all-African church?

After this visit I was asked to do other things, including some Bible teaching, and I did what I could. Then after nine months the penny dropped. I discovered from the little existing literature that I was inside part of a widespread movement of similar strange and unknown groups across Black Africa. I had now been given my subject for research and I dropped my plans to do a Ph.D. on the Moral Rearmament movement through Durham University.

I was now getting inside what called itself The Church of the Lord (Aladura). I found 'aladura' meant praying people, in the Yoruba language in Nigeria. Ten years before, the man on the beach, as a lone Yoruba missionary, had been sent out from Nigeria 800 miles away to Freetown, with only a £1 note in his pocket. Here was the thriving church he had founded.

So what was this body? It was clearly neither Muslim nor some African tribal religion. Could it properly be called a Christian Church, as it claimed to be, or was it some new pagan syncretism beneath a Christian veneer? That was now the question, and I spent the next six years in answering it. The casual contact with the man on the beach, Adeleke Adejobi, had now changed the course of research and, as it proved, of my life.

A lot of time was spent with the congregation in Freetown and I managed to visit most of their other hundred or so congregations scattered over English-speaking West Africa – in Sierra Leone, Liberia, Ghana and Nigeria. Maude was often helping with the research in these travels. It was not easy. I was working under an able African New Testament scholar who was dean of our small faculty of theology. Like most African leaders and missionaries he was hostile to these new movements, even to research about them. "Don't bother with those water people," he said; they used water as a sacramental element for healing and blessing. These bodies embarrassed orthodox mainline African Christians, and they wanted nothing to do with them. So I got no assistance from the university until I had three months' earned study leave just before I left in 1962. Travel till then had all been in vacation time and at my own expense.[1]

The man in the room next door: meeting the Mennonites
On these trips I stayed either with the Church of the Lord people, in the elementary rest house provided for travelling colonial servants on trek, or in the guest houses in larger towns provided by the larger missionary societies for their own travelling members and available for the use of other Christians;

the hotels for expatriates were quite beyond my reach. In this way in Lagos in 1959 I found myself in a room next to a man who in casual conversation turned out to be a lone traveller like myself, an American sent by the Mission Board of a church I had almost never heard of – the Mennonite Church. He was on his way to Eastern Nigeria, to enquire into the bona fides of some unusual request for help that his Board had received from a church with a queer name. Clearly this was another of these independent indigenous bodies.

Edwin Weaver was not an academic doing research, but a missionary retired from long service with Mennonites in India, now sent to make a practical enquiry. Clearly we had overlapping interests and I arranged to keep contact with him. This was the beginning of a long story that has been told elsewhere: how the Mennonite Churches began to help this independent church. They sent Weaver and his wife to open up a new field of service that soon extended to similar bodies in Ghana, and before long to some seven African countries across the continent. Their Indian work was wound down and the Mennonite Board shifted the focus of its mission and concentrated on pioneering among the African independent churches. It remains the leader among Western churches in this new area of mission and ecumenical relations.

I mention all this because it contains a remarkable story that ought to be better known, and because that casual association with a Mennonite that could so easily not have occurred, or not been taken any further, proved crucial for my own further activities in this area and in later quite different areas. I had maintained some contact with Edwin Weaver away over in Nigeria and then had left Sierra Leone and Africa permanently in 1962. In seven years I had done my stint there and I was looking for work in Britain for the rest of my working years, and before I got too old at 51.

For 18 months I was without income, living off the Sierra Leone pension capital I had taken, and getting no job interviews. The only offer I had meant a return to Africa to a new university in Eastern Nigeria; I passed the university enquiry on to Andrew Walls, who had also resigned from Sierra Leone, and he was soon appointed to head its new College of Religion. Meanwhile I wrote up my research on the Aladura Church, not for a Ph.D. but for a Melbourne D.D. for which I had entry through earlier having its bachelor of divinity degree.

During all this there must have been some silent amusement in heaven.

By a string of other seemingly casual events, in late 1963 I found myself teaching back in Africa, in this same university I had rejected in Eastern Nigeria, working again with Andrew Walls in whose appointment I had played a part, and only a half day's drive from where the Mennonite Weavers were now established with a Bible School among a whole range of independent movements.

This proved to be one of the most fruitful periods of my life, in the euphoria of a new university directly sponsored by Dr. Azikiwe, Nigeria's founding President, with virgin territory for research, with the Weavers at work in the field among hosts of these new independent churches, and myself supplying the more academic dimension. The ongoing association that began in this way provided the main support for the Centre for New Religious Movements established nearly 20 years later at the Selly Oak Colleges in Birmingham. There are several distinct Mennonite denominations in North America and on one wonderful safari in 1981, I visited all their seminaries, liberal arts colleges, boards of mission and some congregations, in Canada and the USA. This was to further understanding of this major new mission commitment that both they and I had so 'accidentally' stumbled into.

In all the above the key figure in the Mennonite Board of Mission from the early 1960s was Dr. Wilbert Shenk. Our close association meant that later we both became involved in the newly developing mission of The Gospel and Our Culture in the 1980s in Britain, and then in the 1990s in his own America and my New Zealand. In a real sense, all this, and all that may yet come from such an association, may be traced to that casual encounter with the African man on the beach in Sierra Leone in 1957. And it is to some of the next developments from that meeting that I must now return.

In 1958 Dr. Visser't Hooft, the first and greatest General Secretary of the World Council of Churches, was visiting Freetown as guest of the Sierra Leone Council of Churches. I have already related how I had met him in Geneva 20 years before and I knew he would be interested in a visit to the Church of the Lord.

But this could not be set up through the hostile Christian Council. So I arranged to whisk him off, straight after the morning service for him in the Cathedral, to the 'aladura' service that was already in full swing. He preached most suitably, as the Churches' 'postman', bringing messages around the world. But he was too austere a Dutchman and he left Maude and myself to join in the dancing. Adeleke Adejobi, the man from the beach, led the worship; and no one knew then that within 25 years he would be a member of the Central Committee of the World Council of Churches! But that is anticipating this story.

Can a church include polygamy?

One of the reasons why these bodies had been refused membership of Christian councils was that they did not insist on monogamy. To admit those who tolerated or practised polygamy would destroy the Christian witness of the mainline churches. So I had to examine this objection theologically to see what weight it ought to have in defining what could be called a Christian church in Africa.

In Christian history the best known tests for this purpose occur in the Apostles' Creed: *I believe in one, holy, catholic, apostolic church*. But none of us fulfils these tests; they are norms rather than achievements. Then I realised that while none of the churches in Christian councils passed these tests, yet they excluded a body like the Church of the Lord because it did not pass another practical test that wasn't even in the Apostles' Creed. They were virtually saying: I believe in one, holy, catholic, apostolic, monogamous Church. This was clearly theologically wrong and also hypocritical, since many of their own members were secret polygamists or under discipline on this issue. Or, as Adejobi once put it: White Christians have horizontal polygamy, one wife after another; we Africans have vertical polygamy, several wives together.

So there was some fresh theological thinking to be done, stimulated by these bodies. The immediate application is to say that we must not define the church by any human system, whether in the area of marriage, or economics, or politics. We must not start saying: I believe in one, holy, catholic, apostolic, monogamous, socialist or free market, democratic or whatever, church. In all these areas some systems serve the Kingdom of God more than others, but we cannot use any of them to define or limit the church, and the Christian church has managed to exist under them all.

Now don't get me wrong; I am not weak on monogamy. I was simply ready to accept these churches in spite of any continuing polygamous

(Opposite) Founder of The Church of the Lord (Aladura), Primate Josiah Oshitelu.

practice. So when Maude and I stayed in Nigeria, in the large headquarters and home of the founder of the Church of the Lord, Primate Josiah Oshitelu, and some four of his seven wives were in residence, we were not upset. He, however, was exceptional. He used a verse in Isaiah 4:1, that "in those days seven women shall take hold of one man" – when times were disturbed and men were in short supply. The same practice was justified by the same text from Isaiah by Rua, the Maori prophet-founder of the New Jerusalem community in the heart of the Urewera country in New Zealand in the early years of the 20th century; and no doubt by similar leaders of similar movements elsewhere. Apart from himself and some of the lay members, the ministers, or prophets as they called them, were monogamous.

In our own socially chaotic times the urgent issue is not monogamy versus polygamy, but any ordered system of relations between men and women as against the collapse into promiscuity or temporary partnerships. Polygamy is at least an ordered system. It will be replaced in due time in the course of other social and cultural changes and by permeation of the Christian leaven. The women themselves will see to it; in 1994 it was reported that the women in Papua New Guinea were pressing for polygamy to be made illegal, and this has already happened in some African countries.[2]

I have spent a little time on this one issue to indicate the shake-up in Western theological thinking provided by Christianity in other cultures. I now had to look for other criteria for defining a Christian church, and I cannot go into all that here. Suffice it to say that I concluded that this body was to be accepted as a church, albeit a legalistic one with an inadequate Christology, and an inadequate place for Christ and the cross, atonement and the resurrection. More important was its intention to be Christian, however clouded its achievement might be at the moment. And that goes for all of us.

A continent interacts with Christianity

Now I must try to give you some wider view of these movements. It turns out that there are perhaps some 10,000 of them over most of Black Africa – an independent, indigenous response to Christianity beyond the mission-founded churches. Many are very small, perhaps 20 members, but independent and with an ambitious name. The smallest seems to have been one that tried to register with the Kenyan government; it had a name and an archbishop-founder but no other members yet! The largest, the Kimbanguist Church founded in the then Belgian Congo, must have several million members across a number of African nations.

Over 20 years ago I had a list of 500, their names and addresses, in Ghana alone. The greatest concentration is in Southern Africa where they are known generally as 'Zionists' – over 4000 named varieties with perhaps four million members. Their names alone provide a study. What do you make of the 'Holy Spirit Castor Oil Dead Church'? We smile! But can our own church be so sure that it is dead to sin because it has been purged by the Holy Spirit as if with castor oil? Some good theology there.

Good theology is also found in the fact that in the thousands of churches there are almost none named from their founder or any human being. They seriously aspire to be derived from the true original church of God, not from John Calvin or Martin Luther, or as Wesleyans or Mennonites, not the Pope's church, or derived like the Church of England from Henry VIII and his divorce problems! So you get titles like The Holy Spirit Heavenly Jerusalem in Zion Church of Ethiopia in Africa. These titles are to be taken seriously, and perhaps with a lesson for ourselves.

Not all of these new movements intend to be Christian, even if they have been sparked by interaction with Christianity. Some are prompted to revamp tribal religion and are hostile to Christianity. Some are deliberately syncretistic, combining the old and the new faiths in a new mix.

Now let me briefly survey some characteristic features of those that I would call in some sense churches. First, they are founded in Africa, by Africans, for African peoples to worship in African ways, to meet the felt needs of Africans, but with Christian intent. They are therefore at home with their own drumming and dancing, singing and choruses and clapping, their own church uniforms and freedom from the Western constraints of time. There is still much of what has been received through missions, especially the Bible. But they've done it themselves. And this is tremendously valuable, however shaky or confused in some ways.

Healing of body and mind

Their chief emphasis is upon healing of body and mind. Despite the wonderful advent of modern medicine, there is in fact more sickness in Africa than ever before in its history: vast slums and shanty towns without sanitation, and the strains of coping with two worlds, of Africa and the West, together with all the new social problems and diseases, imported from the West itself; and all this quite apart from AIDS emerging and spreading from within Africa.

So millions look away from the traditional healers to their only available option, the healing ministry of these churches. And much of it works, with prayer, fasting, the use of holy water or oil, and the pastoral support of the believing community. At least some harmful traditional methods are abandoned, and God and nature have a chance. Being focussed on each individual member this provides impressive pastoral care.

Basic cultural changes

In all this there is a remarkable replacement of traditional magic and divination by prayer and faith. What happens to magic and its worldview is far more important than what happens to marriage. This is the basic conversion seen in ancient Israel, and there is sometimes more of it in these despised churches than in mainliners where the old ways survive in secret. In fact the rejection of traditional tribal religion is one of their striking achievements. This even extends to decline of the ancestor cults and funeral ceremonies that are so deeply set in African cultures. God has given us a new set of ancestors, going back through our African founder to the people of the Bible. We are the new Israel, the people of Zion in Africa.

So it is not surprising that many of these churches transcend the boundaries of the tribe and become trans-tribal in remarkable ways. My small Church of the Lord began among the Nigerian Yoruba tribe but spread around dozens of tribes in West Africa, overcoming language and cultural differences, intermarrying, and with prophet-ministers transferred without reference to tribal origin. In a continent beset by tribal conflict, indeed in a world where even Christian Europe displays ethnic purging, this is a tremendous achievement: think of what the Zionists' contribution must mean in South Africa; but it has not received the public recognition it deserves.

The new community of faith provides a new identity and pastoral support when individuals migrate or are unemployed, sick or homeless. And it is also expressed in the development of new holy cities with headquarters, the tomb of the founder, and a resident community of mixed tribal origin, a school, and farming and small industries. So you find Jerusalems, and Zion Cities, and Bethesdas as havens of peace and security, and a source of pride.

Besides the transcendence of tribe there is also the transcendence of the cultural position of women. It is remarkable how many of these churches were founded by young women, around the age of 30 or less. This meant that they were the spiritual superiors even of their husbands or older male members. This astonishing revolution rests on the authority granted to the woman's divine vision or revelation, often in a dream that started her off. I suspect that the startling model of the young unmarried woman missionary who ran a mission station and employed older married men also had something to do with it.

This very general picture applies widely in Black Africa. I have worshipped in a Zionist church out on the open veldt in the Transkei homeland in South Africa, and apart from the language there was almost no difference from a Church of the Lord (Aladura) in the West African tropical bush. And they had never heard of each other.

The tribals' worldwide movements

I was able to trace the origins of the Church of the Lord back to Nigeria and to the great 1918 global 'influenza' epidemic. White man's medicine was powerless this time; churches were closed; people were dying. So some Anglican Nigerians of the Yoruba people set up a prayer group against the plague. They survived and continued to meet. They developed their own ways of worship outside the Anglican structures. By 1925 they had moved off into a separate church called the Cherubim and Seraphim. My Church of the Lord (Aladura) had emerged a little later from this independent praying movement with the same background, under a charismatic Yoruba prophet called Josiah Oshitelu in the area around Ibadan.[3]

In 1963 I had my first return visit to New Zealand and looked up something I had vaguely remembered about the Maori, the Ratana Church. I discovered that Wiremu Ratana was a Christian Maori, with his family sick in the 1918 plague, that he discovered prayer and healing powers, that his family survived, that he continued with his healing and in 1925 formed a separate Ratana Church, Maori-style. The same story, and no possibility of influence either way.

This set me looking for similar interactions in all continents among tribal peoples influenced by Christianity, apart from the particular trauma of that epidemic. And there they were, all over the world, going back to the expansion of European peoples after Columbus, and with similar basic features. Ultimately this led to the special documentation and study centre I was able to establish in the 1980s at the Selly Oak Colleges in Birmingham, England, for dealing with these movements across the whole world; now it is a special research unit attached to the Department of Theology in the university itself.

Now back to 1965 when I was teaching in the University of Nigeria. When Sir Norman Perry (a former Moderator of the New Zealand Presbyterian General Assembly) came from New Zealand for a World Council of Churches meeting in Nigeria I took him to a small Cherubim and Seraphim church in the bush nearby. He is the white authority on the Maori Ringatu religion and he was immediately at home; it was astonishing – he had met it all before; and he has never forgotten that experience.

Ratana, Ringatu, African independent movements, and so one could go on: cargo cults in Melanesia, Peyote cult among North American Indians, Rastafarians in Jamaica (and in our later story), a thousand such movements in the Philippines; all independent indigenous responses to the contact with the Christian Gospel and its Bible.[4]

Persecuting the powerless

Missions and church historians had almost ignored them; or had joined with colonial and other governments to persecute and suppress them. This is a long and painful story. It includes the wrongful sentencing to death for alleged sedition of a new prophet-healer, Simon Kimbangu, in the then Belgian Congo in 1922. He had been a worker in the British Baptist mission and now his public ministry had created a mass movement that rivalled, surpassed, and seemed to threaten their own mission work. But the Baptist missionaries knew he was innocent of any seditious intent. They risked the whole future of their unpopular Protestant mission in the Catholic Congo, by going over the head of the Congo governor with a personal appeal to the King of the Belgians. The sentence was commuted to life imprisonment, but severe persecution of his followers continued for 30 years. Now this church is the largest independent church in Africa, a member of the World Council of Churches, with its chaplains in the army and time on the state radio. But the heroic action of the British missionaries is never told and little known.

I have analysed the trial of the first Nigerian prophet-founder, Garrick

Braid, by the district officer in 1915, set in the context of similar colonial persecution of these misunderstood movements elsewhere in Africa.[5] About the same time, on the other side of the world, the Maori prophet Rua was unlawfully arrested and imprisoned after a shameful trial in Auckland in 1916. In the context of World War I each movement was regarded as seditious or pro-German, both trials showed fear of the indigenous peoples rising against the whites, and in both cases the authorities were determined to get their man, as a disturber of the peace, and manipulated the law to do so. Worse still, in 1949 a High Court judge in New Zealand ordered the destruction of all Supreme Court records of criminal trials before 1929, which included the transcript relating to the police raid on prophet Rua and to his trial. It is interesting to speculate on why this was done.[6]

I have included the story of Garrick Braid because, while this was all before my time, I did have the valuable opportunity of primary research into his story, discovering his baptismal record in a church in his area, the Niger Delta, and reading the colonial officials' reactions in the archives of Eastern Nigeria; in this way I felt present in the movement. While only a small child at the time of prophet Rua, I have travelled in his Urewera country and was led to mention him here because of the remarkable similarity of his story with that of Braid in the same years, but so far away. If this were a story of other notable persecutions of the Maori movements it would include the peaceful Parihaka Maori village in the 1870s, and the wrongful imprisonment on the Chatham Islands of the great Te Kooti, founder of the Ringatu religion; this despite missionary Colenso's impassioned essay of protest, *Fiat Justitia*, of 1871.[7]

I must, however, return to the autobiographical mode. I once thought I was in trouble with the Ghanaian government at the time at the end of the 1950s when President Nkrumah was deporting any critical Western journalists. When travelling up-country with Church of the Lord leaders, I was awakened in the early hours of the morning by a car pulling up, heavy boots tramping up to the door, loud knocking. The day before I had walked in the white-robed procession of church members to the market place of a small town, Nkoranza. There I had been called on by my hosts to preach, without warning or preparation, which is hardly my style; and I had never preached on the streets in my life.

Somehow I found myself preaching on Jesus as the servant of us all, from the story of the foot-washing in John's Gospel. This model actually lies behind the political systems born in what was Christian Europe, whereby the heads of government departments are called 'ministers' and their staffs 'civil servants'. Now I found myself applying this to the way government ministers in Ghana ought to serve their people instead of waxing fat and lording it over them, as was only too common. Afterwards I thought how risky, how close to the bone, this had been in public in Ghana. Now I was sure it was the police, ready to deport me. But it turned out to be only the car driver for that day arriving several hours too early.

A new place in history

I could tell of many persecutions and injustices, including a massacre in South Africa. But let a more recent South African story show how far the tide has turned. In the world press, just after Easter 1994, there appeared a photo of President de Klerk, Nelson Mandela, and Chief Buthelezi, the three most powerful political leaders in South Africa, meeting to pray at Zion City Moriah. This is the headquarters and holy city of the largest independent church in South Africa, Zion Christian Church. I have been there, away up in the northern Transvaal. Each Easter perhaps a million or more Black Africans gather there, and now the politicians and this Church were each taking advantage of the other on such a special occasion, the politicians cultivating a people who can no longer be attacked or ignored. Even these despised movements have played a substantial reconciling part in South Africa.

Twenty years after the Ghanaian false alarm I had experience of the turn-around in government relations. Not far from Zion City Moriah across the border there is the small independent kingdom of Swaziland. It has hosts of Zionist movements and each Good Friday they marched in their vivid and varied uniforms into a great Easter celebration especially for them, in the presence of the Queen Mother and government ministers at her Royal Kraal.

In 1979 I was attending in the crowd, quite informally dressed, simply as the guest of an African lecturer in the national university; unknown to me he had passed a note about my presence to the central party. Without warning I heard my name on the public address system, calling me to come to the microphone and address the gathering. I was more discreet than in Ghana. Since I was then teaching in Aberdeen University I simply brought greetings from the tribes of Scotland, and from the Zionists' opposite numbers, the independent churches in West Africa.

There has been a similar turn-around in the attitudes of most, but not all, of the churches. I had helped Adejobi, the man I met on the beach, to have two years at the Bible Training Institute in Glasgow, which seemed to be the most suitable place for some training – middle of the road and not too sophisticated biblically and theologically.[8] He even managed to get his wife to leave their family behind in Nigeria so that she could join him for his final term and share a little in this new wider world – culturally, not a very African attitude to women. When the founder died in 1966 he became primate of the whole Church of the Lord. Nine years later he went to the Assembly of the World Council of Churches at Nairobi and his church was admitted as a member, along with some other similar bodies for whom he was the spokesman. Then at the next Assembly in Vancouver he was elected to the Central Committee of the World Council of Churches.

These churches have desperately wanted to be accepted by the main Christian body. Now one of them could be said to have arrived. Indeed it soon became almost fashionable to know something about them, and I found myself having to protect them from the stream of curious ecclesiastical tourists – all kinds of tourism corrupt the local culture. But it is a far cry from when I was the first European to take the Church of the Lord seriously and worship with them in Freetown.

In Birmingham there were many new independent churches arriving from Africa or the Caribbean and, as elsewhere, the first problem was finding a building in which to meet. Approaches to local churches for hire of a church hall or the church itself outside service hours were sometimes met sympathetically, but not always without problems. The church and its furniture might not be left tidy as it was, or the advent of a noisy congregation with its drumming and strange costumes on a Sunday afternoon in a quiet suburban neighbourhood did not commend the local congregation to its constituency. An Anglican parish church in Union Grove, Clapham which had offered Sunday afternoon use of the church lost its organist over the issue; he could not stand this heathen drumming in his church.

The University of Birmingham in conjunction with the Selly Oak Colleges sought to help these churches by instituting a University Certificate in Theology, with a curriculum specially designed for their pastors and prophet-leaders, not only locally but over a wide area of the Midlands. Classes were held on Friday nights-Saturdays and in periodical intensive weeks. The highlight was the annual special graduation ceremony for award of the Certificates, Afro-Caribbean style. On one occasion I attended the ceremony when it had been transferred to one of their own churches (bought from a redundant white congregation), and at a certain point when the whole congregation joined in African-style solo thanksgiving dancing, there were the Dean of the Faculty and the Head of the Department dancing amid the rest, still in full academic robes, with white faces conspicuous amid the joyous African countenances – the ivory tower was empty on these occasions. It is good to be able to report such positive stories within a Western society. As I shall relate in Story Seven, ironically the same university administration was rejecting research students from South Africa and refused to publish my protest about this.

What they can teach us

In conclusion, what lessons have I learned from these movements? I have mentioned the theology of the church, and the criteria for defining it. Among others there is a wider view of ecumenism, of the range of our fellow Christian communities.

One way this came home to me was when I was faced with signing up as a minister to go into the proposed united church of Anglicans, Methodists and Presbyterians in Nigeria in 1964. It was a very poor union scheme. The Presbyterians had sold out on their contribution, and I didn't see how I could go along with it.

Then I realized that I had been prepared to be publicly identified with this despised and theologically shaky Church of the Lord, marching in a white gown in their public processions, photographed in the press with them. Why was I not prepared to identify with this united church? Was I waiting for a church good enough for *me* to join? That settled it and I signed up. The Church of the Lord helped me to be much more open and ecumenical than I had been.

I could detail further lessons learned, but I will conclude with one lesson that I still have to work at. The Church of the Lord has some bishops, and dreams figure prominently in African cultures. One bishop exhorted his flock "to learn to dream like a Christian, whose mind is at rest in God and

(Above) The author (left) and Mrs Turner (third from left) with members of The Church of the Lord (Aladura), Nigeria, 1962.

who fears no evil". And so I leave you to ponder upon this Christian wisdom of one of these new African churches.

Just to think upon all that has come, under God's providence, from a casual encounter with a stranger on a beach. Nor has it ceased. Adeleke Adejobi died in 1991; three years later Maude and I received a letter from his family inviting us to become honorary trustees of the Adeleke Adejobi Foundation that the family has set up in his honour and to serve the Church of the Lord (Aladura). Since then I have written a Foreword to a life of Adejobi that has been written by a professional historian in the University of Ife, and I have seen to it that he is included in a major biographical dictionary of Christian missions.

That beach encounter is still working out, linking our lives on this side of the world with a very different church in West Africa, and all within the unpredictable Providence of God. And I think I can now join in the heavenly amusement back in 1954 at my little plan for a cosy life quietly teaching divinity in an education college and training teachers for religious education in England.

The Rastafari

In the previous story I showed how a casual beach encounter led to involvement in new interaction movements between the Christian faith and the tribal peoples in all parts of the world. This next story moves in some depth into one of the most exceptional of these new movements – the Rastafari of Jamaica, and leads me into a prison in New Zealand – as a visitor, let me add!

Jamaican slavery

It is not surprising that the great explosion of such new religious movements in Black Africa should have counterparts in the Black populations of the Caribbean. But there is one fundamental difference: whereas most of the African movements arose in a colonial situation, those in the Caribbean emerged in the situation of slavery, after transportation from homelands they would never see again.

In the African colonies these movements appeared through interaction with Christian missionaries, and under colonial administrators who were for the most part comparatively benevolent, contrary to the bad press colonialism continues to have. But in the Caribbean there was no extensive missionary work and such Christianity as the African slaves absorbed came mostly from colonial chaplains and white masters, some earnestly Christian and benevolent but many depraved and harsh.

Perhaps nowhere in the world, in the modern history of slavery, were conditions worse than in the British settlement of Jamaica. It is almost more than I can endure to read in detail the brutal treatment the slaves received in that colony. That is the background for this next story.

In 1832 slavery was at last abolished in Jamaica. But a century later large numbers were still poor, landless, unemployed; they belonged nowhere, neither to Africa nor to Jamaican established society. So it is not surprising that they latched on to a remarkable Jamaican called Marcus Garvey. In the 1920s he led a large organization spanning Jamaican and American Blacks, with a back-to-Africa vision and the promise of repatriation to the idealized African homelands, through his own Black Star shipping line which later collapsed amid charges of fraud.

Ras Tafari the Ethiopian deliverer

Garvey's followers believed that the Black peoples had been enslaved as a punishment for their sins, but had now served their sentence and Jehovah (they called him 'Jah', from Psalm 68:4) was about to deliver them. Garvey prophesied that 'a black king' was going to arise in Africa to gather the Black peoples together. Hopes for this king were fastened on Ras (= prince) Tafari, the title of the Crown Prince in the ancient independent Black kingdom of Ethiopia. This had been named in the Bible, traced its royal house back to King Solomon and the Queen of Sheba, and had been Christian from New Testament times but had never been a colony. In Jamaica those sharing these hopes of deliverance adapted the name of Rastafari for themselves. In Africa, various new religious movements incorporated the word 'Ethiopian' from the same heroic model into their church titles.

Ras Tafari was the first Ethiopian ruler ever to go abroad, travelling in Europe in 1924 and so becoming widely known. In Jamaica they retained the name of Rastafarians when in 1928 he assumed the title of 'negus' (king) and when two years later the old Empress died he was crowned Emperor of Ethiopia and took the name of Haile Selassie ('Might of the Trinity'). He was seen as the new messiah through whom Jah would now redeem his African peoples. Jah was doing it, and so there was no need to agitate or fight for repatriation.

The Rastafari

Thus the Rastafarians, a new peaceful movement, was born. Its watch-words were 'Back to Africa' and 'Peace and love brother'. Their appearance was somewhat unkempt with their long rope-like hair coils, and they rejected white culture as 'Babylon' the oppressor that would surely fall like its biblical predecessor. They used the King James version of the Bible, and identified with suffering Israel especially during the Babylonian exile; the imprecatory Psalms expressed their modern rejection of all who had oppressed them since their removal from Africa, and Psalm 137 was their favourite, for the identification there was so easy.

One can perhaps understand why Jamaican society feared and persecuted them; but that story cannot be told here. The only ones who ever settled back in Africa were a few score on 500 acres that Haile Selassie gave to them at Sheshamane in 1955; these have persisted there till this day.

I had been able to gather extensive documentation on all this in the Centre for New Religious Movements at the Selly Oak Colleges in Birmingham. During a short time for this purpose in 1976 in Kingston, capital of Jamaica, I managed only one visit away from the bibliographic research in the libraries. I sought out the remnant of a once-famous but now almost extinct body called the Bedwardites – and established my bona fides by showing prophet Bedward's ancient granddaughter and the few followers how they danced in African independent churches! The Rastafari were largely found living in shanties out on the 'Dungle' – the city rubbish dump, and I made no effort to meet them, for it is usually undesirable for a stranger to arrive for brief contact, and then never be heard of again. I have tried, not always successfully, to apply this restraint from becoming an academic tourist when tempting single-contact opportunities occurred in areas of the Peyote cult in the USA and elsewhere.

Rastafari in Birmingham

My knowledge of Rastafari was therefore academic, until the early 1980s. Then it took flesh and blood through a most unlikely link. John Geyer was the minister of the congregation where we worshipped in Birmingham. He had been a theological lecturer, was a notable Old Testament scholar, pretty 'square' both in theology and appearance.

(Opposite) Haile Selassie (1892-1975), crowned Emperor of Ethiopia in 1930, was deposed in 1974. He is revered by Rastafarians as the new messiah for Africa.

One evening, seeking someone who had come into his concerns, he drove over to Handsworth, the area where Caribbean people and Asians lived, and where much had been burnt out in the recent riots. He stopped his car and asked some black youths for directions. They said it was hard to find, so he asked if they minded getting in and showing him the way. They were so astonished at a white man risking them into his car that they began talking together, and he said he would like to come back and talk further. So they met again and this led John Geyer into the Black community of Handsworth, where many were Rastafari, and where he began to be trusted.

I can select only a few of the repercussions of this contact. One Sunday a Rastafari came to morning service of John Geyer's church, explained his faith, and entered into dialogue with the congregation. Later he brought some Rastafari to see their story told in our documentation centre, where I briefly employed a young woman of the Twelve Tribes of Israel, the chief branch of the Rastafari.

The main local development focussed on a Black pirate radio station in Handsworth. The Government had plans for licensing local private stations but nothing ever happened. A Black group, including Rastafarians, set up PCRL, 'Peoples Community Radio Line', and tried repeatedly for a licence. Meanwhile they persisted in broadcasting illegally, around the clock, and developed many community activities for the aged, for unemployed youths, and children. These programmes were invaluable in this deprived and volatile area.

The government department concerned tried to stop this pirate station. But it moved from place to place and divided its technical equipment up into sections easily shifted at short notice, so that in some 40 raids it didn't lose too much. It spent three weeks in an Anglican church until it was located and fled with the equipment out the back as government officials came in the front door; the hospitable vicar was then in trouble with his superiors. When the government brought charges in the courts, against the wishes of the sympathetic police, the also sympathetic magistrates threw the cases out, and PCRL bravely carried on its service in the Black community.

In all this, John Geyer was up front – in the court; bringing the embarrassing question of support for a pirate station before our Church councils; when Rastafari and others were in prison on other accounts he visited or wrote to them, and supported their girlfriends. Some letters of thanks from prisons appeared in our congregational newsletter. They nicknamed him 'John the Godfather', and offered him time on the pirate station!

In the background I was supporting him, against congregational fears that he was being deflected from his ministry. One night he brought the prime mover behind the station to our house so that we could work through the now extensive correspondence with the government in yet another appeal for a licence. And we unsuccessfully sought the support of our local MP; but there was negative political mileage in being involved with Rastafari.

I wish I could tell the rest of this story, but in 1989 I left Birmingham, shortly afterwards John Geyer went to a church in Scotland, and I don't know the sequel. It does, however, illustrate again what can come unexpectedly out of a casual encounter, if one allows it to develop. And for me it was a personal introduction to active Rastafari members, and there I expected to leave it, when I returned to far-off New Zealand. There seem, however, to have been other ideas in heaven.

Rastafari in New Zealand

The story shifts now to my friendship with Sir Norman Perry, who had danced with me in the Cherubim and Seraphim church in Nigeria. He had trained in the former very conservative Bible Training Institute in Auckland, and when his unconventional but highly personal approach to evangelistic work among the Maori found no favour he struck out on his own as an independent missionary. He supported himself by working on their farms, and so became intimate with Maori culture and especially with the Ringatu religion that was strong in his area, and so similar in its worship to the Cherubim and Seraphim we had attended together in Nigeria. Later in a life spent in varied service of the Maori people, including the establishment of production co-operatives, he was knighted.

In the 1980s he established the Mahi Tahi Foundation, out of the limelight but doing notable preventive and rehabilitation work among Maori youth in and out of prisons, and with extensive unpublicised support from the government and the judiciary. In the prison world many young Maori give their religious affiliation as Ratana, Ringatu, or more recently, Rastafari, to the bewilderment of the prison chaplaincies from the mainline churches. The Mahi Tahi Foundation now has established regular voluntary in-prison, Maori-style meetings, prisoners living together with Maori elders (and no prison staff present) over several days in a room converted to a traditional meeting house, to discover their own culture and its sanctions. There have been some striking results among former gang members, and among some Rastafari.

Jamaican Rastafarianism among Maori in New Zealand prisons? How this happened must be sketched. Back in Jamaica the tide of opposition began to turn when Haile Selassie made a state visit there in 1966. The Rastafari could not be excluded and their welcome stole the show at the airport. Then they began producing distinctive styles of music that drew upon both Christian hymn tunes and African drumming traditions.[1] Some of this became known as reggae, and led to a Rastafarian singer, Bob Marley, and his band becoming famous in Jamaica in the 1970s. The bitter struggle between the two political leaders, Manley and Seaga, was expressed in rival gangs of thugs with violence and killings. No one but Bob Marley could have staged a public concert that the two politicians could not afford to ignore, and where he forced them to make peace and shake hands across the top of his head.

Marley's band achieved international fame and came to Auckland in 1979 and made a great hit with Maori youth. Gang members turned into Rastafarians and adopted a whole new reformed lifestyle, which was documented on a television programme that I received at the time on video from the Rev. James Irwin. My sister had also sent me press cuttings, so I knew of the further developments after a Jamaican Rastafari named Hensley Dyer came to New Zealand in 1981 as the leader in Auckland, and married a young Maori woman.

Maori Rastafari in prison

So when I was back in New Zealand in 1989 and Norman Perry enlisted me in his activities I already knew a little of the New Zealand scene. He had arranged for us to go to Wellington that December to a conference of New Zealand prison superintendents on the problem of the high proportion of Maori in prison. He was to explain what was meant when they signed in as 'Ringatu', and I was to have an hour explaining the Rastafarians.

I could not do this when I had had no contact with Rastafarians in New Zealand so I had to hurry up and rectify this. I had great difficulty in finding Hensley Dyer in Auckland, circumventing his unlisted phone number, and

The remnant of Israel shall not do iniquity, nor speak lies, neither shall a deceitful tongue be found in their mouth: for they shall feed and lie down, and none shall make them afraid.

- Zephaniah 3:13

TENASTILLIGN - GREETINGS

in the name of our Lord and Saviour Jesus Christ who in this time reveals himself in the true personality of His Imperial Majesty Emperor Haile Selassie 1st

I BRO JOSEPH 1ST
(as Enock)

of

1 SIS DINAH
(as Miriam)

THE TWELVE TRIBES OF ISRAEL

warmly invite you to a night of

VISION AND HEART COME TOGETHER AS ONE

on FRIDAY 16TH FEBRUARY 1990
at ELLEN MELVILLE HALL (Hall Upstairs),
Cnr of High St and O'Connell St,
Auckland, New Zealand.

7pm till late
Fashion Show 9pm - 10pm
Prime Time 10pm - 12am
Show Time 12am

Admission $8 Adults
$4 Children

Featuring Live

(Above) An invitation to a night of music, fashion and worship organized by New Zealand Rastafarians.

starting from cold on the doorstep when I finally located his house; after much suspicion I was finally invited inside. When he realized I had some knowledge of Rastafari and after he had accepted a book on Marley's reggae music that I had taken with me, we had some good conversation. Then Maude and I and my daughters began to be invited to attend some Rastafari public functions, which were very impressive. This was especially so for their concert and fashion parade one night, displaying their creativity in their own haute couture – even if there were white youth sitting around on the floor smoking marijuana.

Therefore I was able to describe the Twelve Tribes of Israel, the name of the Auckland group, to the prison superintendents as a peaceful community, self-disciplined, self-supporting and industrious. They kept a low profile with their illegal sacramental use of marijuana, and were doing what few others seemed able to do for a number of young Maori men and women.

They were known publicly through their Twelve Tribes of Israel reggae music band, and there was a feature article in the *New Zealand Herald* on this. In November 1990 there was a Rastafarians choir singing on national TV at a peak hour, and they were conducted – wait for it – by a non-Rastafarian Pacific Islander policeman in uniform.

The Auckland Rastafari were authentic and I spoke to some who had visited their small community at Sheshamane in Ethiopia. Hensley Dyer had been there and had also helped found a Rastafari community in Ghana.

The prison superintendents took much of this in, even though I was speaking against the public image and their own experience. These had both been shaped by notorious young Maori gangs on the East Coast of the North Island around Ruatoria, where there was an unemployment rate of 80 percent, and illegal marijuana growing and selling was a major economic support for a deprived area. After one gang member had been to Auckland and been impressed by the Rastafari group there, some young Maori from the gangs had latched on to the Rastafari name and its special use of marijuana, but had still been involved in gang warfare, with arson, horse theft and considerable violence which alienated them from the community.

So there were two groups of Rastafari – the non-representative ones on the East Coast, who were the only ones known to the public and in the prisons, and the genuine ones in Auckland who strongly dissociated themselves from the 'Ruatoria mob'.

'Kidnapping a policeman'

For a number of years, this 'Ruatoria mob' under their leader Christopher Campbell had been in real trouble with the law, and some had served prison sentences. In the early 1980s Campbell had been acquitted in one multi-charge trial, and this had provoked the setting up of a 'self defence' 'Rangers' group on the model of neighbourhood watch, in their turn harassing the Rastafari in Ruatoria where the latter were centred. Both parties complained that the police did not act when offences were reported, although there were four (later five) officers in this small community of some 800, receiving a

$9000 bonus for the Ruatoria location, and one being a brother of Campbell. The Rangers were led by Luke Donnelly, a cousin of Christopher Campbell, whose farm adjoined that of one of Campbell's brothers, and there had been angry slanging matches between them. Donnelly neither drank, smoked, used marijuana nor allowed it to be grown on his land.

This indicates the situation when in 1986 two Rastafari were out on bail on charges before the courts but failed to appear, had warrants issued for their arrest, and fled to a remote hut in the bush along with Campbell. Although they had no warrant concerning Campbell, it seems the police might have been glad to find charges against him also. While at the hut he had some mystical experiences at a nearby sacred pool with waterfall, in which he bathed and felt united with a divine power.

When their location was discovered, Campbell was reported to have been seen with a rifle. The Armed Offenders Squad was mobilized, moved in on the hut overnight, and deployed strategically in two groups armed with rifles and pistols, equipped with radios, smoke canisters and teargas, and supported by a dog-handler and a helicopter. At dawn Campbell was awakened by a loud-hailer in the bush saying they were surrounded by police and demanding that he come out with hands on head. He emerged, fearing for his life, with a rifle and his Bible, saw only the dog-handler who fled into the bush, then he himself tripped and discharged the rusty rifle. The topography was such that he seems to have outflanked a policeman behind a bank, who was concentrating with his rifle on the hut, and had taken him hostage under threat from Campbell's empty rifle.

He took his hostage to the hut, removed all his offensive gear, and emptied all ammunition from the weapons. By now he had discovered two things that upset him greatly. That the hostage (with his face blackened by boot polish) was Laurie Naden, whom he had known all his life, and that his pistol had been loaded with the expanding type of bullets known as dum-dums, something that no civilized police would ever use! His already mystical state of mind then seems to have moved into a semi-hysterical and ranting mode, shouting at the police and sure that he would be killed.

They gave the hostage cigarettes, drink and food, found him a horse, and then the four rode off promising to take him so far and then release him, near a stockyards where the helicopter could pick him up. The trial transcript gives little evidence of what the powerful and over-equipped Armed Offenders Squad was doing, beyond using the loud-hailer and keeping out of harm's way. Of course the three were apprehended in due course and brought to trial. Campbell received an eight-year sentence for 'kidnapping a policeman'! The complexities of the true situation will never be sorted out, especially since a week into the trial Campbell dismissed his defence lawyer and conducted his own defence, causing much trouble for Mr Justice Chilwell.

A leader in prison

In 1990 Campbell was in the new Mangaroa prison near Hastings, where the superintendent at the time was himself a Maori who had been at the Wellington conference. The Maori prisoners had organized themselves into rival groups – the Mongrel Mob and the Rastafari. In the conflict between them for the allegiance of new prisoners, Christopher Campbell had lost his front teeth.

In September 1990 I visited my sister at Havelock North, near Mangaroa. Norman Perry suggested I meet with both the superintendent and Christopher Campbell in Mangaroa. I was able to explain Rastafarianism to the superintendent and his senior staff, and to have an hour in private alone with the Rastafari leader, and met some of his Rastafari 'brothers', all with full facial *moko* or tattoo of Rastafarian symbols or biblical texts. Christopher had RASTAFARI in large letters across his forehead.

The story he told me included a good Anglican upbringing and secondary education at Ngata Memorial College where he had been dux, and then early alienation from family and society as a Black Power gang leader. Later he converted to what he thought was the Rastafari faith through discovery of Bob Marley's music, and he also developed an interest in the Ringatu religion, its founder Te Kooti, and in the prophet Rua – all in that East Coast region, where both these Maori religious leaders had been in violent and quite unjust relations with the government.

When I saw him in September 1990 he was due to be released the next month on parole. He planned to be reconciled to his family and return to the family farm, live quietly, and meditate on his Mt. Zion, the sacred Mount Hikurangi, while awaiting 'the coming of the son of man from the East.' Mt. Hikurangi is in fact the first land to the west of the International Dateline to catch the rays of the rising sun. A few days before I met him he had had a vision of sleeping there in a pup tent and meeting Haile Selassie.

He was clearly seeking a new non-violent way, and he traced this back

(Above) Rua Kenana Hepetipa (fourth from left) and his son Whatu, handcuffed, 1916.

to a vision he had some years before when he 'hit an all-time low' and 'something broke in him' and he had 'given his life to the Lord' – meaning, I presume, Jehovah or Jah, or even but less likely, Haile Selassie. Others with him during this period who believed that he was becoming a changed man included Superintendent Rana Waitai, head of the Gisborne police, the chairman of the Ngati Porou tribal council, Api Mahuika, an unnamed kaumatua (elder) who told this to a television journalist, and Detective Hikawai who figures again below. Donnelly may well have known little of this 'rehabilitation'.[2]

What to make of this from a charming and articulate Maori with forceful personality, good English, well educated and claiming the King James Bible as his authority? Probably no one will ever understand the mixture of social alienation, ancient tribal conflicts, gang warfare, Rastafarian ideology and biblical input that enter into this tragic East Coast story. I joined those mentioned above in belief in both the stature and the sincerity of Christopher Campbell, and saw the prospect of a new day on the East Coast.

Immediately after Christopher's parole, Norman Perry and I had some further contact with the Rastafari in Mangaroa prison. They wrote asking for a copy of the Ringatu worship book, which was sent to them. The Catholic

(Above) The New Zealand Herald *on 29 February 1992 gave full page feature treatment to the events surrounding the Christopher Campbell killing.*

nun who led some chapel services in Mangaroa told me the Rastafari were quieter now. They used to disrupt the services, shouting "Jah", or reading their own Bibles, or wanting to talk endlessly about their beliefs. She now saw their potential for rehabilitation and self-discipline.

Christopher Campbell's killing

Then, on 4 December 1990, some five weeks after coming out on parole, Campbell and four others, three of them Rastafari, were driving past Luke Donnelly's farm. According to the evidence of the car's occupants in the trial transcript, the latter hailed them to come up the farm drive; they then drove up the drive, with Campbell walking ahead. Knowing that a violent argument might develop, he told Mrs Donnelly to phone the police.[3] Donnelly and his wife went inside and he returned with a shotgun. Campbell kept saying "Let us talk," and urging Donnelly to put the gun down. During the argument that ensued Donnelly sent his wife inside for a rifle. With a succession of shots from the shotgun while he was screaming and yelling (according to the Rastafarian Bolingford), he then shattered the windscreen, punctured the radiator and a tyre, and hit Kaihe the driver with pellets as he got out. Then Campbell was shot by Donnelly, both with shotgun and rifle, even after he had fallen to the ground.

At gunpoint Kaihe was ordered by Donnelly to lie on the ground at his feet face down, and the police found the two in this position when they arrived shortly after the shooting. Since neither Donnelly nor his wife gave evidence at the trial, this is the version given by Campbell's associates as recorded in the trial transcript, and supplemented by police evidence from the same source. Campbell died that night on the operating table of Gisborne Hospital, primarily from the shock and loss of blood while he lay unattended before police and ambulance arrived. I felt this deeply and feared that the vicious circle of violence would begin again.

Luke Donnelly was tried for murder. The District Court deposition hearing came six months after the killing, and the trial in the High Court as much as 15 months later. The jury trial lasted seven days, and he was acquitted after pleading self-defence, although all in the car were unarmed and at first only Campbell had actually got out. Donnelly alleges that insults and threats of serious harm had been made by Campbell and his associates a few days before this incident, and it seems he believes these in the light of the Rastafarian record in the district, and he discounted reports of Campbell's change of heart. He walked from the court reportedly saying he was glad he had done it, and would do it again.

I am not too surprised at the astonishing jury verdict, in spite of what would seem to be overwhelming evidence against it. Rastafari had a deservedly notorious image on the East Coast; Christopher Campbell was known as the leader; and any change of heart on his part was not known publicly. And in any case the Rastafarian religion was strange, unknown, and feared, as well as seriously misrepresented by its self-proclaimed local adherents.

Despite what would appear to be a perverse judgment, there is no right of appeal against an acquittal, which could have taken the case outside the public reactions of the East Coast. No jury could be dispassionate in these complex circumstances. This is borne out in the history of earlier strange and unpopular new religious movements, from George Fox and the Quakers to the Mormons, and in the 20th century, to those mentioned in my story of the new movements in Africa, and to the prophet Rua's trial in New Zealand.

Subsequently there was not even a minor firearms charge against a man wielding a loaded rifle and shotgun in the course of an argument with someone unarmed. If I were to use even a harmless athletic starter's pistol to threaten a burglar in my house I would lay myself open to be charged. Before the year was out the police were opposing Donnelly's application for a renewal of the firearms licence they had cancelled after the killing.

Repercussions

The irony is compounded by the verdict of guilty in another Gisborne jury trial, just two months after Donnelly's acquittal. In April 1992 Hata (Raymond) Thompson, one of the two Rastafarian companions in the hut with Campbell, was tried after a delay of nearly two years. He was found guilty of threatening to kill the same Luke Donnelly in a clash in Ruatoria in June 1990, six months *before* the latter killed Campbell. Thompson's version is that in a fracas, Donnelly had tried to gouge his eyes out and he, Thompson, had gone and got a shotgun and marched Donnelly up the main street with the gun under his chin. Donnelly's version of the affray places the onus on the Rastafarians.

Against the background of all these events it appears that some Rastafari did retaliate. Two months after Donnelly's acquittal, his house was burned down while it was unoccupied, and less than three months later a garage he owned met a similar fate, and there were a number of other acts of violence against his property. No one seems to have been charged with these offences, but the possibilities are fairly clear. Then in January 1993 a house belonging to Tom Fox, a supporter of Donnelly, was burned out, although a Rastafarian confessed and was sentenced in this case.

This complex series of events reached its ironic but less violent climax in Ruatoria in October 1993. By this time the irrepressible Donnelly was standing for Parliament in the Gisborne electorate as an independent candidate, with a law and order platform that included longer and harsher prison sentences. When the New Zealand First candidate began campaigning in Ruatoria through a public address system, Donnelly installed his own much louder system three storeys up and drowned out his rivals. The police had to break down the door of the room to take him to the police station for allegedly breaching the peace, but he was released after an hour without charge. A similar incident is reported from Gisborne when New Zealand First leader Winston Peters was the speaker drowned out.

Apart from the arson case above, the local Rastafari as a group had only one small conflict with the police; retaliation for the killing of their leader was deliberately repudiated, and a new leader stepped in. In the month after Campbell's death, Maude and I were staying with Norman and Phyllis Perry in their then home near Opotiki. Norman arranged for Api Mahuika, chairman of the Ngati Porou tribal council (Campbell's tribe), to drive over from Gisborne together with a woman tribal leader, to discuss what might be done for these Maori Rastafari, especially through Mahi Tahi. So I had a chance to explain what genuine Rastafarianism meant.

The most important fact is that the quiet situation continued. You don't hear of it now. Rastafari numbers declined and some are reported to have been 'born again' in a charismatic Christian group. One party of Rastafari trekked across to Opotiki to look over the Mahi Tahi programmes, and a few stayed on to participate. That is real progress. Since then my own concern has been channelled into another outcome of the leader's death.

Suppression of the records

This story raises a number of questions that I have felt compelled to pursue. The first thing is to study the trial itself, which was a public event. To this end I applied to the Registrar of the Court in Gisborne for a transcript of the trial. He replied that this could be released only at the discretion of the trial judge. I applied for this; the judge refused.

A dean and a sub-dean of two faculties of law have both advised that there is no right of public access to the report of a public trial. I was advised to try the Secretary for Justice, with the same result. It is all at the discretion of the trial judge, and from the story as I have reported it one wonders why a judge would use his discretionary powers in this quite legal but also quite disturbing way. And what happens when a judge dies? So where is a member of the public seeking the record of a public trial? And how do those studying law, or lawyers referring to past cases, find out what happened? The *Gisborne Herald* kindly sent me photocopies of its own press reports, day by day, of all proceedings; but that is not an official and full report.

My own church was no help. When I outlined this situation in the course of a paper at the bi-cultural consultation on our Ohope Marae early in 1993, the church leaders, including some Maori, who talk so much about justice to the Maori showed no interest – much less assistance in active following through on a matter of considerable public importance. They didn't want to know. So there I had to leave the matter, not feeling able to pursue it further.

When in 1999, however, a sophisticated white Rastafari, Nandor Tanczos (the name is Hungarian), was elected to Parliament under the MMP system, this offered a new opportunity to secure a transcript of the Donnelly trial. So I wrote to Mr Tanczos, told him the story, and sent an article I had published on Rastafari as a movement and among the Maori. He replied that he would follow my route with an application to see the transcript, but as a Member of Parliament. This apparently made the difference and he received a copy of the transcript, which he has shared with me

Then Mr Tanczos decided he would like to pursue the whole affair further back to the account of Christopher Campbell's trial in 1986; but the Department of Courts in Wellington stalled on this, and wanted reasons for the request. So Mr Tanczos had to approach the Privacy Commissioner for guidance on the information needed to support his request. Then a journalist from the Gisborne area was allowed to copy, even if inadequately, the transcript held by a legal firm involved in the trial. Through his generosity in making a copy for me I have been able to reconstruct the story as above.

As I write, the matter has not gone further than this point, but the repeated secrecy raises questions about the justice system. It took eight years and an oblique approach through an MP for me to secure access to a public record which should be more readily available. Even then, however, the transcript does not include the judge's summing up to the jury, which can be of considerable influence, but of which there is no public record. There are several important matters here awaiting law reform. The main part of my own battle, however, has it seems been won, and the sequel lies beyond this story.

Who are the Rastafari?

Now all this may seem a far cry from Rastafarianism as a religious movement. But it is necessary to have full and accurate information about the course of this new religion among the Maori people, as a case study. And not only Maori, for the Twelve Tribes form of Rastafari has opened to whites; I have met one or two in Auckland, Mr Tanczos is another example, and the mother of a white youth phoned me up from Hamilton concerned about her son being caught up in this, to her, terrible cult.

But what of Rastafarianism abroad? It seems to have spread widely, but not in strength – as among Australian Aborigines, to Japan, and South Africa. Its message applies to all who have been oppressed by Babylon, i.e., by white Western and Christian cultures. In the Western Cape University (then especially for the 'coloured' population) at a courtesy meeting with the Vice-Chancellor he wanted to talk of nothing else than a student who had left to join a Rastafari community not far away at Paarl. Back in Jamaica the 'Back-to-Africa' theme has been transformed into building the African heritage in Jamaica and the Rastafari have become a social reform movement.

And what of Rastafarianism as a religion and in relation to Christianity? A Catholic priest has called it the "most dynamic religious movement in Jamaica".[4] It reveals the moral qualities of being trans-tribal, increasingly trans-racial while maintaining an identity for Caribbean Blacks, non-violent, rejecting or controlling the use of alcohol and tobacco, and advocating a naive ecological concern for the natural state of man – hence the long hair and vegetarianism. The chief moral defect has been the inferior position of women, but that too has been changing rapidly.

Some of our difficulty in seeing it as a religion stems from the lack of admission procedures or clear membership basis, no developed belief system, and no clergy, priests or formal leaders, no set forms of worship or special buildings, and very little ritual – mainly the informal sacramental use of marijuana as the sacred herb given by God, as 'authorized' in the way they read Psalm 104:14.

While white culture and churches are rejected there is no animosity to individual white Christians. There is considerable intellectual or theological activity in protracted sessions known as 'reasonings'. These use much material drawn from the Bible, especially from the imprecatory Psalms such as Psalm 137, and from the Revelation of John on the downfall of Babylon. Identification of this oppressed African diaspora with the suffering people of Israel readily provides one form of identity, and another lies in the belief that each individual contains something of the divine and therefore is to be treated with dignity. Biblical warrant is sought for these Rastafari beliefs, but the incarnation, cross and resurrection of Jesus are of no special account, except as possibly the forerunner for Jesus' return as messiah for the African peoples in the person of Haile Selassie.

It could be briefly described as a form of messianic Judaism developed by people of African descent who see themselves as Black Jews. The movement could not have developed apart from the Christian context of Jamaica, and to that extent it is a Christian derivative. It should be noted that the new religious movements developed in Africa itself are not usually messianic. They operate with founders and leaders known as prophets, called by God but not given the special functions and exalted status of a messiah, as with Haile Selassie. It seems that messianism appears in the more desperate and hopeless situation of an African diaspora.

For myself: I have lost contact in Auckland, after the leader shifted house twice. My interest has been directed to the judicial issues arising from the trial for the killing of Campbell, and that remains an ongoing concern.

Much of this experience has been rather wearing, and I am probably too close to these matters to detect Providence at work. But if I had visited my sister in Havelock North a few weeks later I would not have met Christopher Campbell and not have been involved in these further highly significant and still unsettled issues. Why it has to happen to me, I don't know. The New Zealand section of the story had certainly not been part of my plans for the ninth decade of my life, and if there is any laughter in heaven on this score I am not yet ready to join in.

The 'Moonies'
or the Unification Church

I have been speaking of my experiences with three unpopular new religious movements to which I had neither planned nor sought my introduction. In each case there seems to have been some apparently trivial factor that led unexpectedly into a whole new religious world that I could so easily have missed, but for the hidden leadings of Providence.

Now I want to share something of the fourth experience of this kind, how I came to be deeply involved with the Unification Church. This was founded in Korea by a Korean named Sun Myung Moon; it has been popularly known as the 'Moonies', and under this term it has always had a very bad press.

The 'Third Adam' from Korea

Let me briefly sketch its history. Back in 1936 Moon was a young engineering student with a Presbyterian background in Korea, when he claims he had a vision of Jesus Christ who told him he had a great mission to pursue. At the end of World War II he began preaching in North Korea and was imprisoned and tortured. He was released by United Nations forces in 1950, and made an epic journey on foot back to South Korea.

There in Seoul in 1954 he founded the Holy Spirit Association for the

Unification of World Christianity – the 'Unification Church' for short. In 1957 the scriptures of the church were published: *The Divine Principle.* Written by associates of Moon, this is a remarkably sophisticated work, drawing heavily on the Bible. The Unificationists believe that Christ as the 'second Adam' established only a spiritual Kingdom of God, and that the full restoration of the human race after the Fall recorded in Genesis needed a further messiah, a 'third Adam', to complete the physical aspects of the Kingdom on earth. God chose Korea as the second Israel and the final messiah would arise there. Although never publicly admitted, there is no doubt that the Church believes this has already happened in the person of Sun Myung Moon. Neither Jesus nor Moon is divine, but both are messiahs.

In 1959 Moon sent his first missionaries to Japan and to the USA, in 1964 to Germany, and in 1966 to Britain. A dozen years later members were claimed in 40 countries. Its members were mostly young and well-educated and were supplying a labour force for a remarkable range of business enterprises that provided an economic base. The Church had applied for membership of Christian Councils of Churches in Korea, in the USA and in Britain; all these had refused.

Now in Aberdeen in 1977 I knew little of all this. What I knew came from the media and from horror stories that circulated informally. The dramatic rise of this movement, and some of its spectacular activities such as the mass weddings of thousands of its members at one time, had given the movement a high public profile. This was accentuated in the 1970s by aggressive street evangelism and by fund raising from hawking novelties, sweets, flowers, candles, etc.

The horror stories

It was the horror stories that dominated the public image. These told of impressionable young people inveigled into the movement, then virtually held in captivity, cut off from their families and friends, brainwashed into zombies, and exploited to raise money for the extravagant lifestyle and lust for power of Moon the founder. The Moonies were therefore one more example of the sinister, dangerous 'sects and cults' that arose in the 1960s and flourished in the 1970s – Hare Krishna, Children of God, Transcendental and other Meditationists, Divine Light Mission, Sri Chinmoy, Rajneesh, and other Indian gurus and Babas. The eccentricities, scandals and tragedies of

(Above) Unification Church founder Rev. Sun Myung Moon and his wife wave to 40,000 believers during mass wedding ceremony at Seoul's Olympic Stadium, 25 August 1992.

the 'sects and cults' produced great copy for the media, led to clashes with governments, and raised hysteria and wild gossip among the public, which was then reported as fact by the very media that had created much of it. This was all I had to go on, for a new range of religious movements very different from those like the African ones I had met in the past, and they weren't on my agenda, or so I thought.

My attitude was reinforced about 1977 by a first-hand report that came our way. A New Zealand woman in her 50s had set out on her first overseas tour along with a woman companion. My long-standing friend, Alun Richards, unknown to me had given her our name and address as a port of call in Aberdeen. One day we had a phone call from a stranger giving this unexpected introduction and saying could she see us? So we said to come along that evening.

She was a nice woman and she was bursting to talk about the Moonies, which she did non-stop for several hours. This was her story: she had fallen out with her travel companion in Edinburgh, and being upset and now for the first time on her own, she thought she would make for us in Aberdeen. She had to change trains at Dundee, and went for a cup of tea on the station. A nice young man there must have seen she was a bit distraught and entered into friendly conversation with her. He said he had friends in Aberdeen and he would like her to meet them, and gave her the address.

When she arrived in Aberdeen some of them, nice young people, were already on the station to meet her and invited her to have a cup of tea at their place, which was close by. So instead of phoning us she had gone with them and been intrigued by the community of several races, calling themselves on the gate name-plate 'The Unified Family'. They were Moonies, recently established as a small community in Aberdeen.

They got on so well with their visitor that they invited her to be their guest at a week's seminar at a main centre they had in Dunbar in southern Scotland. She was already somewhat charismatically minded and this seemed to her the new leading of the Spirit in her distressed situation; so off she went with some of them by car back to the other side of Edinburgh, to a big country house near Dunbar. Here she found other guests, and they were all treated royally and led through several days of seminars and singing, while the Moonies expounded their beliefs.

Later in the week, after wearying of the heavy treatment, she had a dream set in an escape scenario and she took this as a further sign from the Spirit that she should leave. They were unhelpful now but she did so and came back to Aberdeen and phoned us straight away. So all this she had to pour out to us in great detail.

Late in the evening I drove her to her hotel, and we never heard from her again. The story had nothing sinister about it, but it certainly confirmed our negative image of the Moonies. It fitted with a phrase we had read about their intensive 'love-bombing' of people.

Encounter at the front door

It would have rested there if it had not been for yet another casual encounter. One evening not long afterwards a young man came to the door selling a religious magazine. I said I was in the religious line myself and had more religious literature than I could handle, but before I could turn him away he began to tell me his story. He was Irish and had scraped through an architecture degree in Dublin, while on hard drugs, with long hair, and then he had set out on a bicycle to ride to India in search of wisdom – a typical specimen of the counter-culture at that time.

While stopped at traffic lights in Paris, young people in a minibus next to him had entered into conversation. He got no further towards India. They were Moonies, and now here he was, a fulltime 'missionary', as he put it, working among the sailors on the ships in port, with short hair, neatly dressed, clean-cut, selling me a Moonie magazine. I must have listened patiently, for he finally, to my shame, gave me a copy of the magazine. He also told me where the Moonie community lived in Aberdeen and invited me to a Sunday morning service there.

Next day I faced some awkward questions. Here was someone obviously rescued from the drug scene. If some stoned youth landed on my doorstep, what would I do? I knew nothing about that world, nor did our nice respectable Church of Scotland congregation. Perhaps there were treatments at the Aberdeen hospitals, but I knew nothing of that. Yet now I did know of someone recently rescued. Would I hand over a drug addict who landed on me to this cured addict, one of those awful Moonies? Yet here he was, rescued by them in a way I could not do.

If I dismissed this as more Moonie manipulation, wasn't I in danger of calling light darkness? – a pretty serious sin in the New Testament. Perhaps we had better find out more, and go down and see what they did on Sunday mornings.

So Maude and I skipped church and did just this. There turned out to be no service that morning so we just chatted with the nice young woman head of the community; she was a mathematics graduate who had pioneered the Aberdeen mission. Throughout our visit a young man sat reading the Bible in the window seat – we learned that he was a doctoral candidate in the University of Aberdeen where I taught. Not much sign of brainwashed zombies that morning.

Some time later we asked the leader and a member to come and have dinner with us and we had a very interesting and what might be called 'spiritual' conversation; but they stayed on and on when the evening was clearly over. Then the penny dropped; I realized they were waiting for some prayer, so I suggested this – 'Before you go'. The leader joined in with a very Christian prayer; and they went.

Developing friendships

This led to increasing contacts and friendship. They asked me to come and talk about African new movements. At this time I needed extensive help at the University in preparing my documentation of the African and all the other new movements in tribal societies for microfilming. So I asked if some of their Aberdeen members who were not resident as fulltime workers, would like to undertake it as a way of raising funds for their activities. We ended up with a team of four for several months: a young unemployed graduate, a young out-of-work house decorator, a housewife and an older man. I could not have had a better team. So I was now involved in funding the Moonies!

Only Professor Andrew Walls in our Department of Religious Studies knew who they were; it would not have been safe to let this be known. Then a young Australian evangelical couple came for a year as volunteers to help in this project, while they learned about new movements in Africa in preparation for going to Nigeria as missionaries. They raised the workforce to six, and got on very well with these 'awful Moonies'; they had of course to know who their workmates were. I believe there was much theological discussion between them when I was not there.

When Maude and I were away for six months in 1980 in the Antipodes the Moonie community offered to care for our garden; they actually wrote to us in New Zealand and reported about the number of languages that had been spoken in the garden while they were keeping it shipshape. And when we left Aberdeen in 1981 for Birmingham they presented us with a Scottish travelling rug and a silver candelabra, for being friendly rather than attacking them like most others. How could we help it? They were such pleasant, spiritually-minded people, full of good works, even if their basic beliefs were far from orthodox Christianity. Of course I had been amassing literature about all this, and I knew pretty well where I stood in relation to the movement; it was no threat to me.

In 1981 we transferred ourselves and the documentation centre on new movements to the Selly Oak Colleges complex in Birmingham. There was a Methodist Church just across the road from us, and so on the first Sunday we went there. After the service a man buttonholed me with some concern: Was I Dr. Turner? Did I know what the Moonies in Aberdeen were saying about me? That they were referring to a friend of theirs, Dr Turner. I am afraid I showed pleasure rather than the alarm that was expected.

I learned later that he was a worried father on the staff at Selly Oak. His son had interrupted doctoral studies (in Aberdeen!) to join the Moonies, and had been sent to America, where he had been through an arranged marriage to a Korean member. I explained later to him, as I did to various naturally alarmed parents, that they ought to be grateful it was the Moonies and not some of the free sex and drug-using cults that were gathering up young people in those decades. At least there was a strict moral discipline here, no alcohol or tobacco, simple living with no self-indulgence, and something that was trying to be Christian, however misguidedly. But I never really got through to that father; I know it was hard for him.

Dangerous friends

More disturbing was a request from the President of the Selly Oak Colleges Federation, Professor John Ferguson, a distinguished scholar and Christian lay leader who had been the main supporter of our transfer to Selly Oak. Despite this being the great centre for mission training and studies in Britain, including a joint centre for Christian-Muslim relationships, he asked me not to bring any Moonies on to the campus. Muslims, yes; Moonies, no.

I had no plans for Moonies on the campus, and as director of the Centre for new Religious Movements this was my field and I knew what I was doing. So I said nothing; but the whole eight years I was at Selly Oak this remained a controversial issue. I discovered that there had been some unfortunate experiences from young, aggressive Moonie missionaries invading some of the college residences in search of student recruits, and this had rightly been objected to. There was also the staff family that felt it had 'lost' a son to the cult.

Friendly relations were developing with the Moonie community in Birmingham and with the national leadership in London. Some of them actually came, inconspicuously, to short courses I ran, although I once found an item on the Colleges' Senatus agenda querying this without any prior reference to me.

My associate staff member in the New Movements Centre was Dr. Jack Thompson. There was such a public hue and cry about the 'menace of the cults' that he and I felt it was safer to arrange a term's course on the subject through the extra-mural department at the nearby University of Birmingham, where I held an honorary research fellowship. Despite all the public interest on the first night only four turned up; the quorum was ten, so the course was cancelled.

The four were so disappointed that we offered to continue it informally without fees, off the university campus. Now one of the four was a local Anglican vicar, and only Jack and I and the other three knew that they were Moonies – the head of their Birmingham house and two national leaders who had driven up over two hours from London. In a public class their own religious position was immaterial, so we said nothing. In view of the Selly Oak situation we could not relocate on campus, so we repaired to the dining room in our flat. There around the table on Thursday evenings for 11 weeks, with the London pair driving up and back each night, and with two more students we picked up quietly at Selly Oak, we had a wonderful time.

We took some of these new movements as case studies. When in about three weeks we came to 'do' the Unification Church I just had to come clean and introduce three of the group as members themselves, who could help us to keep the record straight. The Anglican vicar got quite a shock. But by this time we had established a good group accord, with intelligent participation by the Moonies. The vicar stayed and later said he wouldn't have even started if he had known, but he was so glad he had done so.

Then about 1987 I took part in a national television programme on 'the sects and cults' in relation to the European Parliament, a story I shall tell next time. Then President Ferguson began fielding telephone calls complaining about my supporting those terrible Moonies in the name of the Selly Oak Colleges. He sent me a letter saying he thought my activities were harming the Selly Oak Colleges, and virtually asking me to cease.

This was the crunch point for me. I was not prepared to stay at Selly Oak with a copy of that letter in the files. I was able to show him the text of what I had actually said on television. Although preparation had taken over a day of my time including a visit to London, the selected TV interview lasted 45 seconds and made no mention of any particular cult, much less the Moonies. Nor had any reference been made to the Selly Oak Colleges in introducing me, and I had been rather sorry about the missed publicity for the Colleges.

Poor John Ferguson didn't know which way to look. I said he might like to think about the letter he had sent. Next day I got a note saying the copy had been destroyed; I replied that I had destroyed the letter. In this way it was settled privately, to his credit, and in a thoroughly Christian fashion; but it shows the ramifications of ignorance and hysteria even among highly intelligent and informed Christians.

Despite this small but critical victory, I never really felt comfortable at Selly Oak, for I knew there was intermittent talk behind my back. The worst of it was that no one but John Ferguson and the distressed father ever discussed the problem with me personally.

The controversial conferences

During our last year in Birmingham the two Unification leaders in London suggested that we meet for open discussion about their Church and my Christian faith. Two of them, sometimes three, drove up fortnightly from London for a two-hour-or-more session in our house that I like to think was worthwhile on both sides. It was certainly genuine dialogue between faiths, and there were many other informal and friendly contacts.

I was now receiving invitations to the Unification Church conferences, which provide one example of the way this Church had departed from the ways new and controversial religious sects usually behave. As a sociologist of religion pointed out to me, sects and cults usually stand over against the main Christian community in dogmatic opposition and reject all overtures and theological critique. There was plenty of opposition from the Christian churches, but the Unificationists were turning the other cheek and inviting people like myself to be their guests at expenses-paid conferences and seminars, openly discussing theological and other themes, and their beliefs in relation to ours, without any possibility of our being manipulated – certainly as far as I was concerned.

My first invitation was to a conference at Bristol. My research colleague at Aberdeen refused to come with me because they were Moonies. It was interesting and in no way threatening. The practical arrangements were in the hands of a team of students who, together with the Korean principal, had come over for the purpose from their theological seminary near New York. My main criticism was the way we were paired off at mealtimes, each with a Moonie student neighbour who talked incessantly about it all and showed no interest in us. It was surprising to find the student paired off with me was a young woman from Christchurch, New Zealand! Pretty efficient management somewhere?

The emphasis upon theological education was also uncharacteristic of new sects. Bright young men were being sent for doctoral study at the top theological American schools such as Harvard and Chicago. So when I was in America in 1979 I was able to visit the Unification Church seminary as a guest for several days and so to see for myself. Here were able students, a good library, a faculty drawn mainly from scholarly non-Unificationists, and extensive premises that had been bought from a Catholic monastic order. Yet such was the prejudice that they spent a decade trying to get registration from the State of New York as an educational institution. And I doubt if the blockage was due to the subject taught by my neighbour – at one faculty lunch when I asked him what he taught he told me it was the martial arts! These of course are also spiritual exercises in Asian cultures.

Two incidents from the seminary visit remain vivid for me. One was when an academic psychotherapist came to lecture on the then recent tragedy of the People's cult mass suicide at Jonestown in Guyana. The lecturer had been involved in rehabilitating some of the few survivors. He likened that cult to the Unification Church in its unquestioning following of an authoritarian leader. This produced vigorous objection from the Moonie students, who asserted their own freedom of thought and action. One asked me if I thought he looked as though he had been brainwashed.

The other incident emerged at the very early daily chapel worship. The day before I left, one of the students had been invited to meet his parents at a motel not far away. There he had been kidnapped by the professional paid de-programmers who in those years commonly operated for distressed parents, and the son was being held prisoner in the motel. Someone had called the state troopers, who were standing by but not interfering. The student had managed to get a phone call through to the seminary in the middle of the night, and now we were praying for him. I never learned the outcome, as I had to leave that morning; but it was an insight into the opposition to the Moonies and the methods being used by the anti-cult movement. And I heard other personal stories from adult students who likewise had been kidnapped by their families and held prisoner in places like remote farmhouses, until they had escaped. In one case the kidnapping family were, of all things, Quakers!

Now back to the Unification Church's conferences. That same year in America I was able to let them pay for my travel across the States and for the 5-star hotel venue for a conference in Los Angeles on the unity of the sciences. That is just what it was, with top scientists, and some Nobel Prize winners, including the neurologist Sir John Eccles who had worked with me in starting the University Bookshop 35 years before in Dunedin. The Moonies hosted it and participated on the level with everyone else. When a few years later I asked why they had these conferences in such expensive hotels, I was told that more modest establishments usually refused a booking when they discovered it was the Moonies, but the top ones couldn't care less who used them, and would rent to the devil himself.

In the 1980s I went to four more conferences at their expense. Each was different. One in Italy was explicitly to expound their position systematically over several days; that wasn't new to me by then, and became rather boring, except for the half-day trip we were given around Rome. At the other three I had to earn my passage by reading an academic paper. The one in London was on religious freedom,[1] and this is the theme of the stories following upon this one. At the conference in Puerto Rico I gave a paper on the new African religious movements in relation to national development.[2] In New Jersey the paper was on tribal or primal religions as 'Humanity's common religious heritage'. Twice I met the founder Sun Myung Moon formally, heard him speak to the conference, and was not impressed. How could the figure I saw inspire this movement?

Whether to accept or reject these all-expenses-paid invitations to Unification Church academic conferences became a subject of hot discussion in the academic world in the 1980s. I stopped accepting invitations after I had been the rounds of the different kinds of conference, and learned all I could. In any case the church has not been able to maintain largesse on this scale, although an incredible variety of gatherings continued on every possible theme.

A financial mystery

How the Unification Church finances these and other expensive operations remains somewhat of a mystery to me. I have mentioned the extensive street selling by a captive labour force of highly motivated young people living on a pittance.

A student in their seminary told me how they went out in twos over weekends into small American towns and covered the town between them, selling house by house until run out of town by the local police chief for lack of a hawker's licence. This was to pay their own seminary fees. Another example came my way at the conference I went to in Italy. One of the Moonie hosts was a very impressive young New Zealander who was busy on the side buying large numbers of silk scarves in nearby Rome, as lightweight merchandise he could take back by air for selling in Nigeria, where he was then in charge of their work.

I believe there are substantial industrial enterprises within the booming economies of Korea and Japan – metal fabrication, marble ornaments, ginseng tea, etc. There have been remarkable business enterprises in the USA such as deep-sea fishing boat building, coupled with tuna fishing, then fish processing and finally seafood restaurants. David, the son of the Selly Oak Colleges family, who had reached advanced studies in science, was put on to developing a soft drink that would be an alternative to Coca-Cola and Pepsi. And by the way, before I left Selly Oak he brought his charming Korean wife over from America for a happy reconciliation with his parents.

There were other small scale industries such as printing in Britain, but I could never fathom how all this could finance these expensive conferences, buy the large New Yorker Hotel where I had once attended a huge American academic convention, or launch a major newspaper, *The Washington Times*, to rival the world-renowned *Washington Post*. I suggest nothing sinister; I just don't know. And *The Washington Times* continued as a serious newspaper, rather like the *Christian Science Monitor* from the Christian Science Church.

Unificationists in New Zealand

Once or twice I have mentioned New Zealand. So what of this movement there? It arrived during the great Unification Church missionary activity of the 1970s, and at one stage it had a fairly public profile, but it has never taken off in this country. In 1980 I saw something of it at a community house they had in Wellington, and heard the story of an ex-Moonie who wasn't negative about his experience.

Then one day I was in the office of the editor of the Presbyterian Church magazine, and there on his desk was a large photo of Sun Myung Moon. He was about to publish the story of a naive young New Zealander who had been caught up by the Moonies in California, and then 'escaped' to tell his horror story. Now I knew two things. That the Moonies in California were the Church at its worst, and that an ex-member of a religious body, especially one of these sects, is widely recognised as the least reliable of witnesses. They are usually busy excusing their having belonged by blaming, not themselves, but the former community for having deceived them, brain-washed them, or whatever.[3]

So I asked the editor if he thought it was the job of a church paper to publish this sort of stuff? How would he like it if the world learned about the Presbyterian Church mainly from those who had left it in some anger? – 'Why I left the Presbyterian Church'. He went ahead nevertheless, but he did also publish later a brief interview with me in which I could offer a more balanced picture; but one can seldom overtake the smear image.

When in 1989 we came back permanently to live in Auckland I found that the Unificationsts were quite small fry in the seething religious stewpot that is Auckland. There might not be more than 50 to 100 members in the whole country.

I have already told of the Moonies being one of the two unpopular religious bodies that came to see us off at the airport when we left Britain in 1989. That was the pleasant end of the chapter, and I had no great desire to become further involved with the Unification Church, unless there was some real reason. The local Church, however, had got wind of our arrival and was soon in touch. A charming mother and daughter visited us and we were sent invitations to functions, and for a year or so we were supplied with their quite interesting tabloid *Unification News*. The headquarters community lives in St. Stephen's Avenue, Parnell, Auckland, in a large house that used to be the summer residence of Queen Salote of Tonga. One night we went to dine with them and had a most enjoyable and 'spiritual', as it were, evening with an impressive line-up of nationalities.

Defending the Moonies

In 1991 they told me about eight of their missionary members being wrongly held in prison in Thailand, and would I help by writing to the Chief of Police there as an academic able to vouch for the respectability of the movement. About this same time I had been approached by the British section as an academic knowing the Church to write in support of their appeal against the refusal of the authorities to grant Sun Myung Moon a visa to visit his Church in Britain, on the grounds of 'the risk to public security'. I knew this to be prejudice and nonsense, and wrote a strong letter in support of the appeal, which was rightly successful; a fuller account will appear in the next chapter.

Even before all this I had an earlier experience of defending Moon himself when I was sure that the United States government had set out to 'get' him. An easy method is to bring charges of tax evasion, and in this the government was successful. I will be relating this more fully in a later story, but I knew well the propensity of governments to persecute these bodies, so I had no qualms about supporting those I knew something about on such occasions.

International 'front' organizations

One of the features of the Unification Church is the formation of an ever-new range of international bodies with high-sounding names and agendas, and often with non-members well-known to the public holding some nominal office in the organization or sponsoring it and speaking on its behalf, usually fairly platitudinously. This resembles the use of public figures I have already noted in MRA. The conferences referred to were often organized in the name of one of these high-sounding bodies.

I suppose I was condoning all this when in 1996 I agreed to speak for the 'Inter-Religious Federation for World Peace' in a public meeting hall at a seminar on 'Sexual Purity – an Urgent Response to a Growing Crisis'. I knew the source of the invitation was a member of the Church, and the response telephone was its own number. I was to be given an hour on 'Gender and Sexuality', and as I had been writing publicly in this area and was involved in the issue I accepted another opportunity to serve 'the cause', even if provided by the Moonies. It was a well-attended and useful meeting.

Married by Moon[4]

Shortly afterwards Maude and I received an invitation to attend the Church centre for the Auckland section of the vast international marriage blessing ceremony to be conducted by Moon himself in Korea, and by satellite for all other countries where there were Unification communities – a predicted 360,000 couples, which I knew had to be merely a symbolic figure. With some reluctance against over-developing our relationship we finally accepted, and went off in our best clothes.

The Parnell house was buzzing with people and activity as before any wedding, much less a group one. Immediately, uncomprehending what it was all about, we were hustled upstairs where the Korean head of the community was waiting to put us through a ritual that involved exchanging small glasses of wine with each other. It turned out that this 'Holy Wine Ceremony' was an initial rite for all marriage blessing participants, and we had been late for the group ritual and had been given our own ceremony. I should have recognised much earlier from my reading what was under way. Then to downstairs where I was left in the hall and given a flower spray, while Maude was at once taken away into a room from which she was shown out shortly afterwards dressed like all the other brides. It all happened faster than I could take it in.

By this time I realized that we were not being treated as guests with some guest rituals, but as participants in the wedding. When I tried to point this out and withdraw no one had time to listen to my feeble protests, and we were swept along with some 20 other couples in wedding attire into the main ceremony. By this time only a violent public scene could have avoided this participation. So we had our marriage blessed, re-blessed or renewed or whatever by Sun Myung Moon himself, who appeared on the television screen at appropriate moments. For much of the ceremony the couples stood, but we (as oldies) were kindly told that we could sit throughout. There was a large Polynesian couple in front of us, and when the video cameraman came down the aisle recording the occasion I shrank down behind the two in front to minimize any appearance in the visual record that might be used for all sorts of purposes.

A changing story

We have not heard from them for a year or so now. I doubt if the Unification Church as such has much future in New Zealand or elsewhere. Its recruitment pool in the youth of the counter-culture of the 1960s and 70s has dried up. This is the era of somewhat older people being drawn into less organised and endlessly variegated New Age movements, both inside and outside the churches.

The Unification Church itself has changed much over the nearly three decades during which I have known it. It no longer raises funds by street selling, or offers such a range of expenses-paid conferences, or retains the controversial public profile it had when kidnappings occurred allegedly both ways, and brainwashing and de-programming were the regular media charges. Its internal organization has changed, and many members have passed through its ranks, some grateful for the experience and others bitterly critical.

One of these is the British leader I have known best, who has already appeared in the Birmingham part of this story, and whose German wife and young family spent a day with us before we left Britain. Since then we have exchanged the annual 'Christmas letter' and kept in touch in other ways. Now he tells me that he has been out of the Church for two years, not so much on account of its teaching, but rather because of disagreement with the financial operations and demands and the founder's leadership. One wonders how he stood some of its practices for well over two decades, but we are all in that situation in various ways with our own churches – none of which are quite good enough (as I have noted in my second story) for some of us!

I have told the story of my own contact, experiences and reflections. It appears that since I have been out of effective contact especially in the period 1995-1999 there have been further and major changes in the naming, the structure, the location and the activities and teachings of the movement.[5] Some of these are mind-boggling, such as the financial rescue of the University of Bridgeport, Connecticut, that gives the Church a majority shareholding, and the initiative in founding there a centre combining Western and Eastern medicine. This university planned to work with the Sun Moon University in South Korea as the beginnings of a World University Foundation.

This university will also help to shift the focus from North to South America, by working with a grandiose plan for New Hope East Garden in the vast undeveloped areas in the heart of the continent, the Matto Grosso do Sul around where Brazil, Bolivia and Paraguay meet.[6] This will become the beginning point for the Kingdom of God on Earth. Moon's imagination and nerve never seem to fail, and time and again little more is heard of some of these schemes, and at other times astonishingly they do come to some fruition, as with the *Washington Times*.

Recent developments in teaching about relations with angels and the spirit world are too weird and complex to be set out here. They include blessings for ancestors, akin to the Mormon baptisms on behalf of the dead;

blessings to allow the spirit of a deceased spouse to return to live with the surviving partner; messages from deceased Church leaders printed now as canonical texts, and their interviews with Lenin, Stalin and Hitler as representatives of the wicked, who are now to be released from Hell. When I knew the Church the spirit theme was well out of sight and these would appear to be somewhat desperate developments, especially after the death of Moon's son in a car crash in 1984.

There has also been tragedy and scandal associated with Moon's own family: a divorced son and subsequent 'revelations' published by the former daughter-in-law; a family suicide, drug abuse and other charges; and the hovering problem of a successor for Moon, who was 80 in 2000.

Despite these alleged later developments, I have no cause to withdraw from the positive relation I had with the Church some time back, or the efforts I made in its defence, which form the substance of the next story.

So there it stands. In Britain I sought to keep the door open in mission towards the Unificationists as I knew them then, and to get some traffic flowing, even if the Selly Oak mission centre kept trying to close it off. Now I am happy, for the time being, to settle for the present less intimate relationship; my hands are full elsewhere. Whether Providence finds this amusing or not, in view of what may lie up the Providential sleeve, I know not. At the moment it is not my business.

Religious Persecution in Britain

I have been telling stories about new, strange or unpopular religious movements – firstly Moral Rearmament, then the indigenous independent churches in Africa, thirdly the Rastafarians, and lastly the Unification Church or Moonies. In each case opposition occurred, ranging from minor harassment to violent persecution. Now I want to tell in more detail the harassment story as I have encountered it for the last of these movements, the Unificationists.

The great century of religious persecution

Firstly, a moment's reflection on some of the paradoxical features of this fantastic 20th century. Never before has such attention been given to human rights, including the rights to freedom of religious belief and practice. This could be one reason why this has been the great century of religious innovation. Despite the predictions that religion was dying out, there has never been such a continuing efflorescence of new and varied religious movements.

In spite of all we may read about mediaeval Europe, the Catholic Inquisition, torture and burnings at the stake, and *Fox's Book of Martyrs* (once common in Protestant homes) – there has never been a century with so much savage religious persecution as the 20th. Think of the Jews under the Nazis, the Baha'i and Christians in Iran, of all religions in Marxist areas and still of Christians in China, of both Muslims and Hindus at the time of the division of India and since, of Jehovah's Witnesses in Malawi, of Christians in Uganda under Amin, of Protestants in Colombia a generation ago. Even Australia and New Zealand within the last two decades will be mentioned in the next story I shall tell.

These stories refer only to the cruder, more violent forms. There are endless forms of harassment, discrimination, and misrepresentation which are harder to identify and destroy, but are nevertheless real and wrong. It was this sort of thing that first came to my attention during my early encounters with the Moonies in Aberdeen.

Petty official discrimination

Like anyone else wanting to sell items door-to-door, the Unification Church in Aberdeen applied to the Chief Constable for the necessary routine 'pedlar's licence'. The applicant was the doctoral candidate in science whose parents at the Selly Oak Colleges I later discovered were so worried. He was refused by the police. He appealed to the courts, unsuccessfully. The sole reasons given for the refusal were that he was a member of the Unification Church and members of the public had complained about this church to the Chief Constable. The magistrate described the Moonies' tactics as 'a foot in the door' to gain access to people and their homes, and it seems people needed public protection from such a risk. What of freedom of religion when what amounts to a business licence depends on the religion of the applicant and its popularity or unpopularity in the community, this reputation itself dependent on rumour and gossip? Scottish history, I should think, has seen a great deal of complaining of one church against another!

The Moonies were establishing themselves by 'Boy Scout' kinds of good works, but these were always opposed. They arranged to entertain some old folks in a Church of Scotland home with songs and games, but when the matron found out 'who they were' she cancelled it. They held a Christmas fair and from the proceeds sent some parcels for Christmas to lonely old ladies in a Salvation Army home – until London headquarters ordered their return.

One school holidays in Torry, a rather run-down suburb of Aberdeen, they organised some of the children roaming the streets to play a few games on one of the open grassed places. First they got them picking up the rubbish and broken glass, until a policeman arrived and ordered them to stop. He had received telephone complaints about them. The Moonie leader told me that he politely asked the policeman if they should replace all the broken glass where they had found it!

'Ban the Moonies'

To 'Ban the Moonies' seemed to become a regular policy everywhere. In the town of Rosyth there was a musical festival planned in aid of the Scottish Society for Autistic Children. Local members of the Unification Church had musical talents and had organized a band, so their leader, George Robertson, offered to give a concert in the parish church hall. The minister, who knew his religious affiliation, agreed; but when the festival committee learned that 'this nice young man who had made the offer' was a member of the Unification Church they banned the concert at five days' notice, and returned the ticket money. As the disappointed leader said: "I don't go round with a label round my neck saying: 'Beware, I'm a Moonie'." Then the festival committee learned that this same versatile Mr. Robertson was billed to give a 15-minute spot of 'song and storytelling' at a fund-raising Scots Night in the Rosyth Hotel on the intervening Friday. So they banned him there also.

Scottish Church uncertainties

Besides this pettiness there was one better response. The Unification Church mission activities in Scotland led to the Church of Scotland Committee on Doctrine setting up a panel to report on the theological position of the Unification Church. Its convener was the Rev. Dr. Iain Torrance, one of the well-known Torrance theological family. The report was non-aggressive, thorough and fair – deciding that in no sense could this be called a *Christian* church.

I agreed entirely with the report and also with its calm tone. So I wrote to *Life and Work*, the Church journal, supporting the report but asking the 'so what?' question – how do we now relate to these Unificationists? I was most unhappy about their harassment in Aberdeen, while I was exploring relationships with them there, and as I thought fruitfully. After havering nervously in a letter to me and consulting his editorial advisory committee, the editor printed a couple of selections that did not amount to much. This was the same editor who in his retirement I have already reported under a decade later as reversing his original opposition to Moral Rearmament.

The Unificationists were not treated so even-handedly when they were naive enough to write to the declining north of Scotland Episcopal Church diocese inquiring whether they had any redundant churches for sale! They got their answer publicly in a scathing attack in the diocesan journal, from the dean of the diocese, with all the usual misrepresentation. I don't know if the letter received a direct response.

Television slander

Of course the press had a field day with anything that could be found about the Moonies, and the headlines almost always added more smear to them. This was happening all over Britain as the church spread in the 1970s. Now I don't expect too much indignation at these small incidents, but I tell them as straws in the winds that were soon to blow in gale force. And I was being prepared for the more turbulent times.

One of the first gusts came in a documentary programme by British independent Television on 'The Moonies', early in 1980. A few years before, I had been involved with the BBC as a consultant in their production of one of the 13-part series 'The Long Search', on the religions of the world. I had been impressed with the thoroughness and fairness of the production and with its results. The Independent Television programme was a shocking parody, a shameful attack, unscientific in its research as a documentary, and incorrect in its 'facts'. Knowing what I did of the Moonies at first hand, I could not let this pass and retain my own self-respect.

So I wrote a detailed critique to the ITV management. I pointed out that the well-known authority on this church, Dr Eileen Barker of London, had not been used, and that the Archbishop of Canterbury, poor man, and some local vicar who had appeared with a horror story, were not authorities. Only highly emotional distressed parents were shown, not the other parents happy to have their family members rescued from the drug scene by the Moonies, the context in which I had first encountered them.

What goaded me into action was the presentation of a Dr. Clark, described as a psychiatrist 'from Harvard University', who slammed 'the cults' in general, and showed no knowledge whatsoever of the Moonies. Now I knew several things about all this. First, that Dr. Clark was only part-time and very loosely associated with Harvard Medical School. Secondly, that just over two months before, he had been rapped over the knuckles by the state medical disciplinary board for rash diagnosis of mental illness, simply on the basis of religious affiliation. I have a copy of the disciplinary board's letter about this. So much for the ITV's 'expert' from Harvard.

Further, it so happened that only a few months before this I had been lecturing at the Harvard University Divinity School and staying in its residence, and had seized the opportunity to find out about the Unification Church doctoral candidates studying there. It turned out there were eight of them, and the Dean of the School told me how satisfactory they were. In addition that week's Divinity School student newspaper had a very positive article about the Moonies in their midst. What would you think of me, if knowing all this, I kept silent? What would I think of myself? Therefore I wrote my strong critique.

At least I had the satisfaction of forcing the Director-General of ITV, Sir Brian Young himself, to write a three-page stubborn defence in answer to my critique, almost none of which he accepted.

The Daily Mail libel

Later in the same year, 1980, the Moonies became regular national headline news. The mass-market national newspaper, the *Daily Mail*, set out to 'get' the Moonies as safe to attack as a major denomination would not be – good media sport! They charged them with brainwashing and breaking up families, in lurid headlines supported by sensational stories.

They misjudged their victim. The Church brought a libel action against the Daily Mail, and they fought with such determination that it became the longest and most expensive libel action in British legal history – for six months it fed the national headlines. One is reminded again of what was then the longest trial in New Zealand legal history, the 47-day case against prophet Rua. Why is it that new religious movements present such problems? – although these are nothing to the reports in the next story of legal struggles up to 20 years long.

In my experience I had found no signs of brainwashing, and the charge of breaking up families could be levelled at every religion in the world where one family member is converted to another faith. Jesus himself recognised this. Christian missions have been causing just as much consternation in Muslim or Hindu or other families when they 'lose' one member through conversion to the Christian faith. In Aberdeen I knew that one year every British member of the Unification Church team there had gone home to spend Christmas with his or her family.

The libel trial judge was calm and fair. Twelve parents appeared in support of the Unification Church. Dr. Eileen Barker, the British scholar at the London School of Economics, had made the major study of the Moonies and she specifically denied the brainwashing charges. And yet the jury found in favour of the *Daily Mail* – i.e. that its charges were true. Costs of about £1 million were awarded against the Moonies. Here is another example to add to those we have already examined, of the impossibility of justice for controversial religious movements through trial by jury.

The Church immediately appealed, especially on the grounds that the judge had misdirected the jury by raising the question of the truth or otherwise of Unification Church theology. This was not the issue, and in any case is never a matter for the courts to decide. They also lost the appeal, and had to find the money. I was satisfied that once again justice in the much-admired British legal system had seriously miscarried.

The only minor satisfaction the Unification Church ever received was six years later. The Press Council, set up to handle libel charges against the press, censured the *Daily Mail* for its still on-going campaign against the Moonies. It had recently published a story of a young man who had killed a fellow patient in a psychiatric institution, under the headline: 'Ex-Moonie Turned Killer'. It could perhaps equally have read 'Ex-Sunday School Teacher' or 'Boy Scout Leader'. The slander was obvious and baseless.

Fortunately – or providentially? – I was in New Zealand for some months in 1980, when the Unification Church solicitors wrote asking if I would appear on their behalf as a professional witness in the libel case. Clearly it would not have made any difference, as they secured someone with much greater prestige (if with less direct experience of the Moonies) – Professor of Religious Studies, Ninian Smart. I would have had to agree to testify, and that would have made things even more difficult for me when I transferred later the same year to the Selly Oak Colleges in Birmingham.

I would also have found myself opposite a witness for the *Daily Mail* in the person of a theologian whose position I share and whom I respect – the convener of the panel that drew up the Church of Scotland's doctrinal report on the Moonies, the Rev. Dr. Iain Torrance. I have the full 20-page transcript of his cross-examination by counsel for both the Unification Church and the *Daily Mail*, along with the interjections by the judge.

His testimony was quite irrelevant to the issues about brainwashing and destroying families. It debated whether the Unificationists were entitled to call themselves 'Christian' and how to define this, the very question the Church of Scotland doctrinal committee under his convenership had properly and fairly dealt with – great stuff for theologians, but not for the law courts, where it should have been ruled out as irrelevant. Think of trying to decide this in court about the Christian Science Church, or the Mormons: 'The Church of Jesus Christ of Latter-Day Saints'. By the time I went to Birmingham in 1981 he was on the staff of The Queen's (Theological) College there, and my relationships with the Moonies was not exactly helpful in getting to know him.

The loss of the libel case gave confidence to all those critical of the Unification Church, and the Church was now buffeted from all directions. The jury had included a recommendation that the Church should be investigated as being a political organization and not really a religion. This shows how little they had learned during the trial. MPs were pressured by parents who disagreed with their grown-up children joining the Church; 180 MPs signed a motion to be put down in the House of Commons, demanding the removal of the charitable status of the Unification Church.

There was pressure on the Department of Health to condemn the Church as doing damage to the physical and mental health of its members. The Home Office was exhorted to refuse visas to members from abroad seeking to visit Britain. It became something of a hysterical witch-hunt, and the popular press kept on baying for blood.

The chief pressure was placed on a statutory body known as the Charity Commissioners, who registered charitable organisations and administered the charity tax law. I wrote to the Chief Charity Commissioner in 1981, the year after the television encounter. I simply spoke from my experience of the Unification Church and in opposition to the pressures being put on the Commissioners. I hope it helped a little.

Anyway the Charity Commission was able to withstand the mounting pressure, even when this came from the Attorney-General himself. Fortunately the Commission answers directly to Parliament, or obeys the Court of Chancery, and it simply said 'no' to the Attorney-General's repeated requests.

Moonies case fails after witness is found hanged

Court action against the Moonies is being dropped by the Government after the alleged murder of its key witness, it was revealed last ni[...]

By NIGEL HASTILOW

Mr Wilshire said later that Miss Martin left the Moonies in 1984 and had moved to live in Falmouth,

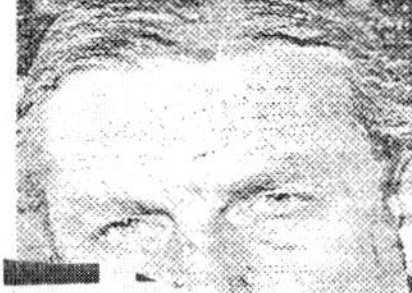

has proved to be i[...] ciently reliable."

MPs of all partie[...] cised the decisi[...] called for the Hor[...] tary, Mr Dougla[...] carry out an ur[...] of charity law[...]

The Ho[...] later th[...]

CITY STI[...]L SALES BAN ON MOONIES

MOONIES AND 'MIND CONTROL'

THE son of a wealthy publisher who became a [...] the Moonies in [...] High Court

Murder claim at Moonie inquest

MOONIES SECT 'LIKE MAGGOT' SAYS WOMAN

THE daughter of a wealthy landowner wh[...] gave his estate to the Moonies reli[...] [se]ct yesterday described the sect in [...]maggot[...]

[fr]om an [...]ents be[...]ed a sui-[...]x-Moonie [...]d frequent Richard van 25-year-old

Girl's father in protest over verdict

[co]urt fight

[...]ver Moonies

Comm[...]

Ex-Moonie girl was murdered, says MP

[...] SENSATIONAL alle[g]ation that a former [M]oonie disciple was [mur]dered b[...]

By GORDON GREIG and MARGARET HENFIELD

anything to the murder of Sonia Martin who was to be a key witness in this case? A lot of people have been

(Above) Britain's tabloid press indulged in a feeding frenzy with stories about the Moonies, many of which were based on hearsay or mere fabrication. The legal repercussions lasted for years.

On an earlier occasion the Commission had removed the charitable and tax-exempt status of a religious body, the Exclusive Brethren. They had appealed and the Commission had been forced to restore the charitable status. It had come to realize what a hornet's nest would be stirred up if it tried defining religion and excluding any one body. It simply said that it had no grounds for action.

The Attorney-General fiasco

This went on for three years (the characteristic dragging out of such cases that we have already noted) until in December 1984 the Attorney-General took the extreme step of appealing to the Court of Chancery against the Charity Commissioners' refusal to act. The Chancery Court is the senior Division of the High Court and possesses the ablest judges in the justice system. The appeal was supported by a nine-point indictment of the Unification Church. If successful it would be the end of the road for the Church in Britain, and with global repercussions.

So the Moonies once again had to face a protracted and expensive legal operation. They assembled a defence team, consisting of some of their own bright younger members including Mark Brann, himself a lawyer. To these were added an eminent Queen's counsel and two other barristers, one of whom was the acknowledged British expert on charity law. Then three academics were added from the USA and three academics from Britain – Professor Ninian Smart, the doyen of religious studies in Britain, Dr. Bryan Wilson the doyen of sociology of the sects in Britain and Sub-Warden of the prestigious All Souls' College, Oxford, and myself. I don't think I was the doyen of anything, just a knowledgeable and friendly academic in religious studies.

I did not enjoy the prospect of being cross-examined in defence of the Moonies by clever lawyers in the Court of Chancery in London. This would be the end, for some of my Selly Oak colleagues. But, as I told in the previous story, by this time I had established relations of friendship and trust with the leaders of the Unification Church. Now that they were in trouble what kind of friendship would it be if I were to say: "Sorry, friends! You'll have to fight this battle on your own. I can't afford to get mixed up publicly in it. I'll have to sever relations for a while. Let us pick up again when it's over. But the best of luck to you." I had no option but to join the defence team.

You see, it was nothing to do with the beliefs or with the practices of the Unificationists. So long as the practices were within the law this Church was as much entitled to religious freedom and charitable status as a religion, as my own church. And it was free to hold any theological views it liked, however bizarre, just as I was. That is what I was defending, religious liberty, theirs and mine. Dr. Bryan Wilson was a well-known unbeliever, and Professor Smart was a layman and philosopher rather than a theologian. So I was rather proud to find myself the only representative of the British churches in the defence team, even if those churches might want to repudiate me if they had known what I was doing.

It is hard to describe the next three years during which the case was not brought to court. The defence team met for a long residential weekend and divided among us up the various themes in the nine charges, to work out the rebuttals. I was allotted two themes. First, that the Church engaged in public deception, both by calling itself Christian and by not disclosing its identity at all points in its activities. Thus it should always have first proclaimed that it was the Moonies who were engaging in those harmless good deeds in Aberdeen.

Then my second assignment was allied to this – that it had a secret and sinister hidden teaching, and it was deceiving people by hiding this until they were caught up in the movement. In each case it meant I had to explore the theme in the history of religions in general, including Christianity, and then show that the Unificationists were not doing anything so unusual or irregular after all. It was not difficult to do this and it became a very interesting exercise. The evidence then had to be set forth as part of an affidavit sworn before a Commissioner of Oaths and included in the vast defence dossier. One would then be cross-examined about it in the witness box at the trial.

The Attorney-General was of course likewise collecting witnesses, experts, and affidavits, to support the charges. To our astonishment he enlisted my friend Dr. Eileen Barker, the acknowledged expert researcher on the Moonies. She simply said she had been asked and did not mind which side she appeared on since she would simply tell the truth anyway, and she did not think what she had to say would prove much good for the attack.

Plaintiffs' and defendants' affidavits were exchanged, and it was some-what surprising to receive an affidavit for the Attorney-General from

Professor Stewart Sutherland. He was then Professor of the History and Philosophy of Religion in King's College, University of London, where they had an embryonic centre for the study of new religions, of which he was the nominal director. He had visited me in my centre in Birmingham, so we were of the nature of 'buddies' in the business.

This was a little embarrassing so I wrote to him saying I hoped it would not upset our buddyhood, or words to that effect. He replied friendly-like – that we each had to do what we had to do! More amazing was the content of his affidavit. In attempting to show that the Moonies were deceptive in claiming to be Christian he showed little understanding – as most of us thought – of the nature of Christianity itself. Some of his friends said to me that they didn't know what had come over him. Nevertheless he shortly afterwards became Principal of King's College (1985), and later Vice-Chancellor first of the University of London (1990), and then of the University of Edinburgh (1994), and inevitably received a knighthood.[1]

Equally surprising was a 32-page affidavit from the Rev. Dean Kelly, Director for Religious Liberty for over a quarter century for the National Council of Churches in the USA. This was a splendid authoritative statement, and of course was for the Moonies' defence.

The years 1985, 1986 and 1987 were full of anxiety, suspense, expenditure and further work for the Unification Church and the defence team. There were preliminary hearings, court decisions as to whether evidence was admissible from the USA, changes in the charges, and therefore in the defence materials. Finally it looked as though the case would commence in April 1988, and that it might well last six months, three and a half years after the charges had been laid! The Moonies were wearied, and their opponents were constantly asking questions in both the House of Commons and in the Lords as to why they had not long since been charged and dealt with.

In the meantime there was a new Attorney-General. Then there was a dramatic denouement. On 3 February 1988 the new Attorney-General announced in the House of Commons that he had decided after exhaustive investigation to drop the case! Amid the ensuing uproar he gave two reasons. There was not sufficient reliable evidence to proceed; and he had now been advised that there was a real possibility of being unsuccessful in a protracted and very expensive case. Of course, the professional legal department of the British Government should have made sure of this before it went to court and did this great injustice to the Unification Church. But the Attorney-General included in his announcement the statement that the Unification Church "must now as a matter of law be regarded as a religion".

An uncertain victory

Then all hell broke loose among the enemies of the Church. Individual Members of Parliament put down motions; Lord Denning, a former Lord Chancellor or head of the judiciary, demanded that the law be changed; the House of Lords spent two hours debating it the following week, and a motion was put down in the General Synod of the Church of England deploring the Moonies' continuing charitable status, and this showing complete ignorance of the history of this issue as well as of the Unification Church itself. And the press went wild.

It so happened that just at this same time a 25-year-old woman from a broken home, who had once been a member of this Church for a short period, was found hanged from a road signpost in Devon. Almost certainly it was suicide; but this was manna for the media. Screaming headlines explained why the Attorney-General had dropped the case: the Moonies had murdered one of his key witnesses. I have copies of these press headlines: 'Moonies Case fails after Witness is found hanged'; 'Ex-Moonie Girl was Murdered'. This was libellous.

There was no interest in the actual and genuine reasons the Attorney-General had given for dropping the case. Another common explanation was to blame the British Council of Churches for not having supported the Attorney-General! A scapegoat had to be found, and anything but the plain truth, as printed in the parliamentary record, Hansard. It was not a pleasant spectacle in Britain, the alleged home of justice and tolerance.

I was immensely relieved at being saved a court cross-examination. And as for the Unification Church – it was the first break they'd had. And then they experienced a better side of British justice, for the Crown had to pay the legal and other costs the Church had incurred in defending itself against this wrongful prosecution. I never learned what the appropriate court finally decided on, but it must have been of the order of a million pounds. In addition, the preparations for the trial had cost the Crown itself a similar amount of taxpayers' money.

A few weeks after the dropping of the case the Unification Church held a Thanksgiving Service at which Kenneth Cracknell, the British Council of Churches Secretary for Relations with People of Other Faiths (who had worked closely with me), gave an address celebrating a victory for religious freedom in Britain. Those who had been involved in the defence team had a celebratory dinner in London on the first anniversary of the Attorney-General's announcement in the House of Commons, not long before we left for New Zealand; I was glad I was still there for that.

I cannot help but add a small incident here. I got to know quite well Mark Brann, the Unification Church lawyer member who organized the defence team. In the early 1990s I had a letter from him saying he had been on a Church visit to Korea and while out jogging in the hills had met another jogger from New Zealand! This turned out to be theologian Alan Torrance from Dunedin while at a conference in Korea, a cousin of the testifier for the prosecution in the *Daily Mail* case. They discovered this mutual acquaintance in New Zealand.

Keeping Moon out of Britain

There is but one further chapter – so far – to add to this wretched story of harassment and persecution. It concerns the visits of the founder, Sun Myung Moon, to Britain. From 1965 to 1978 he had made a number of visits without difficulty. Then in 1978, after he had been admitted on a two-week visa, the Home Office refused an application for extension of stay.

The story then becomes confused. Moon appealed to the relevant adjudicator. Among other distinguished supporters of the appeal was the Aberdeen University Physics Professor, R.V. Jones, who had been one of the scientific masterminds behind Britain's secret 'scientific war' against Germany in the 1940s. The appeal was successful, but the Home Office ignored the result and still refused extensions, and Moon left the country without it being resolved. It was at the time of the mounting public hysteria about the Moonies, leading to the events I have already described.

Then in 1990 I received a letter in New Zealand from the Church's solicitors, asking if I would write in support of another appeal on the same issue. Late in 1989 Moon had been refused an entry visa outright. The reason given referred to "the probable public reaction to his presence...in the light of the adverse publicity surrounding both him and the Unification Church

[and] in the light of the applicant's character and conduct, his exclusion from the United Kingdom would be conducive to the public good."

This of course was the same old harassment from a Government that had learned nothing from the Attorney-General's experience less than two years previously. It was all the more ironical when we learned that the Catholic University de La Plata in South America had recently awarded Moon an honorary doctorate, and later in 1990 Moon was to spend two hours in conference with Gorbachev in Moscow! I have already said that this Church broke all the rules and achieved the totally unbelievable – it had not been exactly popular with Catholic authorities, and it had been virulently anti-communist. But now his mere entry into Britain was judged to [and I quote] "have considerable political repercussions", "resurrect anxieties" and lead to "demonstrations against his presence here".

Moon appealed. I wrote as requested, along no doubt with a number of others. The appeal was successful. I have in front of me the six-page judgment, finishing with: "I direct that the Entrance Clearance applied for be issued." But how the Moonies have had to work for plain, basic religious freedom to go about their lawful affairs, time after time. This becomes more than harassment; it is continuing persecution.

Or, the other way of putting it, how much religious discrimination and persecution still occur in the most developed societies, even after centuries of Christian input. And how oblivious the Christian churches can be; some of them have had to fight for their own religious freedom in the past, but how oblivious they can be to the denial of religious liberty for others under their very noses today. And this is the theme I shall pursue further in the next story, at the level of the European Parliament itself.

Note

I have continued in the autobiographical genre by confining this story of persecution of the Unification Church in Britain to where I have been person-ally involved, or very close to the evidence. I feel constrained, however, to add two items I have before me on the similar persecution of the same church in Australia, and of another church in New Zealand, reports that will not be widely available:

1. *The Moonies, the Media and Religious Persecution*, a 14-page essay by Gregory Tillett of the Department of Religious Studies of the University of

Sydney, published by The Peace Academy of Australia Publishing House, PO Box 752, Canberra, Australia, in 1982. This is a fully documented account of individual cases.

2. *The Jerangle Affair*, 129 well-documented pages by Romilly Fraser, who gave me a copy in New Zealand and whose reliability I have reason to accept; published it seems by the Unification Church in Australia in 1979. This tells the story of a new Moonie community attempting to settle in Jerangle, a small country town in New South Wales, and how (among many other things) the local ministers' association rejected any discussion, they were refused a building permit, spied on by the media from helicopters, attacked by arson and scrub fire, and denigrated in Parliament.

3. The same author has also written and self-published in 1978 *The God Squad*, an appalling, documented story of physical attack by government departments on the small rural community of another body, the Full Gospel Mission, in north Canterbury, New Zealand. These provide comment on our supposedly tolerant and secular Western and post-Christian societies, and I shall refer again to the latter.

Political Persecution of Religion
by Modern Western Governments

The last story told of my involvement in the defence of a small, unpopular, new religious movement, the Unification Church, better known as the 'Moonies'. That story had a happy ending – the ignominious and expensive defeat of a British government bent on religious persecution.

Mormons and MRA in Britain

Let me now offer a few reflections on the British record in dealing with this sticky problem of religion. One could go back to the 16th century and rehearse the struggle for religious freedom in Britain, until it seemed to be over by the 19th century with the emancipation of Jews, Catholics and Dissenters. But the 20th century shows that it is never over. There are four British examples that may be briefly offered.

In 1910 there was a 'Mormon scare' fomented by the press with allegations of white slave trading in British girls to provide wives for American Mormons. There were riots or violent reactions against Mormons in some 11 cities. In fact Mormons had repudiated polygamy some two decades previously; nevertheless there was a call for all Mormon missionaries in Britain to be expelled. A government enquiry in 1911 found no basis for the charges, and in 1913 the Home Secretary affirmed support for religious freedom and tolerance concerning Mormons. The Home Secretary was none other than the young but, even then, formidable Winston Churchill. Then World War I intervened, and Americans including the Mormon missionaries were withdrawn to the USA.

Tolerance had won, at least officially, but not for long. Soon after the War, in 1919, the Mormons naturally wanted to restore their missionary force in Britain. A precarious coalition government, fearing continuing anti-Mormon hostility, used the excuse of shortage of shipping to limit the number admitted to four. So Mormon members of the U.S. Senate charged the British government with discrimination against American citizens on the grounds of religion. The Government gave in, and there was almost no trouble.

In the first of these stories I related something of the opposition to the Moral Rearmament movement. One political example occurred early in World War II, in 1940, when the Minister of Labour, Aneurin Bevan (himself an atheist), insisted on including certain MRA fulltime workers, their 'ministers', in the national call-up. He was opposed in both Houses of Parliament. But being himself essential to the war effort, he threatened to resign and got his way. It seems a minor matter to lead to a resignation threat; but this shows the extent to which deep and irrational feeling can focus on a minor religious movement.

Just after World War II another atheist in the Commons, Tom Driberg, who was a life-long bitter enemy of MRA, strongly opposed entry permits for MRA workers from abroad. He didn't get his way. The Home Secretary refused to discriminate on religious grounds; another small victory for tolerance.

Scientologists' battles: 12 years in Britain, 20 in Italy

But it was a vulnerable victory. In 1968 the Church of Scientology was harassed by the British Government. Although it was a Labour government, which might have been expected to be more liberal, getting uptight about the Scientologists, in June the Home Secretary and the Minister of Health had banned anyone entering Britain to study or work with Scientology, and they planned to publish a White Paper (Government statement) exposing the Scientologists. The back-room bungling confusion on the subject is revealed later in the published diaries of Richard Crossman,[1] another Cabinet minister, who insisted that there must first be an inquiry into the information that had been collected, or that this should simply be given to the Daily Mirror and left at that!

In October Crossman himself became Secretary of State for the Health and Social Security Departments and set about setting up an inquiry, with much discussion as to who should undertake it. Finally on 16 January 1969, after over six months havering, Sir John Foster was announced as a one-man Commission of Inquiry. He was a scholarly barrister, and former Conservative MP, known for his independence. As Crossman's diary comments: "Scientology, one hopes, has been cleared up for the moment."

Nevertheless it took *three years* for the very thorough report to appear. This recommended firmly against the government ban. Then it took *another nine years* and a petition from 92 Members of Parliament before the ban was actually lifted in 1980, 12 years later! In the meantime, the Scientologists had appealed at great expense through every possible legal channel, right up to the European Commission on Human Rights. They had also been so savagely and gratuitously attacked by a judge during a case involving one of their members in the high court that even the sober journal, *The Economist*, wrote an editorial entitled 'His Lordship Plays God'.

Interestingly enough at the same time, New Zealand seems to have joined in a world scare about Scientologists. In 1969 the government set up a Commission of Inquiry into Scientology in the country. The two members were Sir Guy Powles (the Ombudsman) and E. V. Dumbleton (a retired newspaper editor). They uncovered some unsavoury material but nothing of great substance. The chief witnesses in defence of the Scientologists were Sir James and Lady Joan Hort of Auckland; presumably such respectable figures made it a little awkward! The Commission contented itself with giving some stern advice to the Scientologists, but made no recommendations for any legislation or government action. New Zealand seemed more relaxed than the British government.

I never had much to do with the Scientologists, nor wanted it, as they scarcely seemed to be a religion, and were not in my special category related to tribal cultures. In the 1980s one of their senior long-time members, a charming woman in her 50s, came from their headquarters and spent a day visiting our Centre for New Religious Movements at the Selly Oak Colleges; we had a pleasant day and when I took her to the Selly Oak rail station for the train back to London she warmly kissed me goodbye. That would have done me no good with my colleagues at the Colleges, as I explained a story or two ago.

Nor did it alter my decision to refuse an invitation to speak at a rally they were organizing in London's Trafalgar Square in defence of religious freedom; and another invitation to visit their headquarters in Sussex. It *may* have influenced my agreement in 1987 to write at their request to the President of Italy, drawing attention to repeated police raids on the Scientologists in Italy, with unlikely charges of drug-trafficking and other crimes. The real reason for the official attacks was more likely to be influence by the phonier sectors of the psychotherapy professions, which Scientologists have long specialised in exposing – and not without some good cause. The President never replied.

The police investigations had begun as far back as 1979, and went on until 1993 when the Milan courts ruled that the Church of Scientology was not a religion, and not entitled to the associated legal privileges. The Appeal Court upheld the negative verdict on this and other charges. In 1995 this decision was sent back to the Appeal Court by the Italian Supreme Court for reconsideration on the grounds that the earlier decisions were based on a too narrow and theistic definition of religion that would, for example, exclude Buddhism. In 1996 the Milan Appeal Court again found the Scientologists guilty, but this was annulled by the Supreme Court, which sent the case back once more with a long disquisition on the nature of religion. Then on 5 October 2000 the Milan Court, deciding on the same case for the third time, finally found in favour of the Scientologists. I presume their Church has survived in Italy amid this legal jungle, despite the penalty of such legal costs; these movements have to get pretty tough.

Hindus, Exclusive Brethren, Unificationists again...

Lest I appear as a bit of a sucker for the sects, let me add that I turned down a request for help from the Hindu Temples' Association after an attack from the BBC on the Hindu-related Hare Krishna movement. I thought the BBC had acted outrageously and told the Temples' Association so; but I did not feel called to help a body of which I knew so little, especially when I was already so deeply involved with the Unificationists' troubles with the government related in the previous story.

It was in this same period of the 1970s and 80s that the British government again succumbed to pressures. This time it came from ex-members of an older 19th century religious movement, the Exclusive Brethren, seeking to remove their charitable status as a religion, and as such presumed to be 'for the public benefit', one of the interpretations of religion for charitable purposes. A government judicial enquiry found against the Brethren and the Charity Commissioners reluctantly complied. But the Brethren appealed in the High Court, the government did not even defend the case, and the Brethren won back their status. That was in 1981 and helps to explain why the Charity Commissioners, as I have told, stood so firmly against the Attorney-General and in support of the Unification Church three years later.

The latter Church has been beset by opposition, often from Governments and public bodies, in divers parts of the world. I will mention only one more of these, the hounding of a Unificationist student organization, the Collegiate Association for the Research of Principles, known as CARP, which extended to Russia in 1992. This began in the Peoples' Court of St. Petersburg in July 1995, without the proper legal procedures, and ordered the dissolution of CARP as harmful to State and people of Russia, together with a fine of US$6 million.

With great courage, Galina A. Krylova, a leading Russian attorney specializing in religious freedom which is guaranteed under the new Constitution, has fought the case through every possible legal and illegal move by the St. Petersburg courts, the national Justice Department, and organized anti-cult hate groups. Finally she took it to the Russian Supreme Court in Moscow, and on 5 November 1999 the Chief Judge read the verdict: "The two suits brought by the Justice Department and by the public prosecutor to liquidate CARP because CARP allegedly violated the laws of Russia and their own by-laws... are dismissed". Both prosecution and CARP were stunned. This is a great victory for freedom of conscience in the former Soviet Union.[2]

'Getting' Moon on tax evasion

As I related in the previous story the Moonies were experiencing more than their share of religious harassment in Britain, but also in many other countries, of which we have just looked at Russia. A new ploy was one of the oldest in the book – government charges of tax evasion. It was used in France in 1984 when the head of the Unificationists was charged with tax fraud of about

US$0.8 million – on the grounds that it was a business and not a religion.

The major example occurred in the USA. In 1982 the founder, Sun Myung Moon, was arraigned by the IRS for tax evasion over three years amounting to the trifling sum of US$7300. I understand there was an internal Justice Department ruling that criminal tax cases are not brought to court for sums under $7500. The tax authorities treated Moon as the personal owner of the large funds he held on behalf of his Unification Church; as Church funds they would normally be exempt from tax. Although Korea had no extradition treaty with the USA, Moon voluntarily returned to stand trial.

The Church employed a professional and expensive research firm to survey the attitudes and prejudices of the community of that court area, and from which a jury would be drawn, and demonstrated that there would be no possibility of justice from a jury trial. Moon therefore exercised his right to choose trial by judge alone, rather than by an inevitably prejudiced jury. The State strongly opposed this and a jury trial it was, at district court level, with the inevitable conviction, a fine of $25,000 and a jail sentence of 18 months.

Then strange things happened. Every Catholic bishop and many other church leaders in the USA realised that their church money and property were often or partly held in their own names as the top church officer; therefore they were just as liable as Moon! So when the latter appealed, support for him flooded in from ecclesiastical quarters that had been bitterly opposed to the Moonies. Catholic bishops, the National Council of Churches, Presbyterians and Baptists, the Mormons and many others including secular organizations such as the American Civil Liberties Union wrote to the court through the procedure known as *amicus curiae* ('friend of the court'), which is not interference with justice but aimed to facilitate it by giving the judge the fullest possible information, to be used at the judge's own discretion.

Upon request by the Church I gladly wrote my own letter as an *amicus curiae*. Despite scores of these from a remarkably wide range of religious and other bodies they made no difference. The appeal was lost, the Supreme Court refused leave to appeal further, and Moon served 13 months as a model prisoner, and made some converts from among the other inmates. I have no doubt that quarters in the US Government had set out to 'get' him, and by a shameful injustice they had succeeded. They also succeeded in making a martyr of him among his followers and in rallying his former enemies, if not to his side, at least to his case.[3]

European Parliament joins in

All these stories of persecution overlap in the time of the late 1970s and early 80s. I tell them partly to supply the background to the main story I shall now relate, the persecution of all the so-called 'new sects and cults' between about 1981 and 1984 – by no less a body than the European Parliament. Here yet again was something in which I was unable to avoid involvement.

Since World War II and the reconciliation between France and Germany, in which, as I have mentioned, Moral Rearmament played some part, a range of new pan-European institutions has developed. This reversed the nationalistic fragmentation of Europe that marks the last six centuries. It is the great Western political development of the 20th century and it includes a body called the European Parliament, which meets at Brussels and Strasbourg. Its parliamentarians, 'MEPs', are directly elected from 567 constituencies spread over the 12 member countries, with more countries added since the time of my involvement. Although only consultative at this stage, there has been a later move to give it some mandatory powers.

In the late 1970s the European Parliament was under continuous lobbying from those hostile to the new religious movements, to 'do something' about these sinister bodies. Nothing much came of it until about 1981 when one of the 87 British MEPs, Richard Cottrell, the member for the Bristol constituency, took up the cause. He himself was a journalist without any religious interest, but there would be voting mileage in an apparently popular cause. He was also a kind of secretary to one of the Europarliament's standing committees with the intimidating name of 'Committee on Youth, Culture, Education, Information and Sport' – nothing less! So for entry into this field he had the term 'Youth' as a mandate, and the Committee as an instrument. The aim was control of these movements, with a particular animus towards the Unificationists. So in mid-1982 the Europarliament Assembly referred complaints received specifically against the Moonies, to this Committee.

Late that year the Unification Church gave me my first news of all this and sought my help. Like most others in Britain I knew and cared little about the European Parliament; British voting turnout has been as low as 38 percent. So I made little response to their evident concern. Then they told me of another member of the above Committee with the long name, Mr Richard Simmonds, who was not sympathetic to the Cottrell attack. He was MEP for the constituency next to mine and living close at hand. So I wrote to him with something of my concern and as a result he came and visited our Centre in January 1983, and we had a very sensible conversation about the issue. He turned out to be an active Anglican church member.

He brought me a draft version of the resolution Richard Cottrell was preparing for the Europarliament Assembly, and asked me to write a critique of it. He then sent this to his colleague, Cottrell, who wrote directly to me with his defence against my criticisms. We exchanged critiques and replies in a series of letters into March, when he started merely acknowledging my missives. So there was no more discussion; I had no incentive to do more.

Then about September a Euro-election was coming up. Our own MEP, Norvela Forster, announced a campaign meeting right in the main meeting hall at the Selly Oak Colleges. I had some incentive to go along; I meant to ask about the Cottrell development at question time, but as usual left it too late and the meeting was closed. But I did approach her afterwards and asked if she could tell me what was happening about the Cottrell Resolution. She had never heard of it, not being on that particular Committee, but she said she would find out. Three months went by, nothing happened and I left it at that. Or so I thought, while I guess heaven smiled away at my relief.

Facing the Cottrell Report

Maude and I were busy preparing to visit South Africa for several months, after an invitation to speak at the opening and closing of the annual conference of the South African Missiological Society. We planned to stay on for a holiday in a seaside house offered to us by Afrikaner friends. Then on the eve of our departure early in January 1984 a packet arrived from my MEP with the latest draft of the Cottrell proposals and other literature. It was shoved away in the baggage, and there it remained until January obligations were over and we settled in for a wonderful three and a half weeks in a lovely house in a remote spot on the Natal coast, with no phone but with a pick-up vehicle at our disposal.

Then at last I read the Cottrell draft statement. And the penny that

Providence knew was suspended in front of me dropped with a clang! There were proposals here that were simply preposterous, by way of 'indiscriminate discrimination' against the 'sects and cults', which were vaguely identified as 'Certain new religious movements'. These proposals were therefore so indiscriminate and ill-framed that they could apply equally to my own church. The United Reformed Church in England could be called a new religious movement, since it had been established about a decade previously from the older Presbyterian and Congregational Churches. Many other newer Christian bodies could also be so described. The alarm was sounded for many of us, just as it had been for the orthodox churches in the American tax charges against Sun Myung Moon. Self-interest alone should arouse concern; but as I shall show there were many other problematic features.

It was now February 1984 and the Cottrell proposals would be going to the General Assembly of the European Parliament for adoption within two or three months. Did anyone in the British churches know what was going on? Not to my knowledge; so I sent off an aerogramme letter (Oh for e-mails then) to Kenneth Cracknell, the secretary of the British Council of Churches Committee for Relations with People of Other Faiths. I knew him well as a warm supporter of 'my' Centre at the Selly Oak Colleges. I said I hoped the British Council of Churches had been monitoring these developments. It turned out that they hadn't – they were quite ignorant of it all.

Let me simply quote how Kenneth Cracknell described it in an article a year later: "I looked at the 15-point set of proposals... called 'criteria' in assessing these new religious movements... called Voluntary Guidelines. Let me pick out just three that struck me at the time. 'Persons under the age of majority should not be induced, on becoming a member of the movement, to make a solemn long-term commitment that will determine the course of their life'; 'Movements may not extract permanent commitment from potential recruits, for example, students or tourists who are visitors to a country in which they are not resident'; and 'Such movements shall be required by law to inform the competent authorities of the address or whereabouts of individual members.' "

"Now these voluntary guidelines... [Cracknell continued] were full of words like 'must not' or 'may not'. This did not sound particularly voluntary... But worst of all... nowhere... was a new religious movement defined... All sorts of alarm bells started ringing."

So Kenneth Cracknell took the Cottrell draft proposals to the Executive of the British Council of Churches meeting a few weeks later. They agreed entirely with his assessment, and on 4 April sent a letter to all 567 MEPs expressing their grave concern over these developments. On 7 May I sent a letter to all 87 British MEPs, laying it on fairly thickly as a bit of an expert in this field, and there were other individuals and bodies of various faiths who wrote in alarm.

In the meantime the Legal Affairs Committee of the Europarliament had – incredibly – checked and passed the proposals, and on 21 March Cottrell's originating Committee with the long name had adopted them by 13 to 0, with one abstention. I hoped this was Richards Simmonds, with whom I had first discussed it all. In the final draft the overall title had been changed to the even vaguer and more contentious: "New organizations working under cover of religious freedoms", whatever that means.

When the British Council of Churches opposition became public many other religious organisations in Britain woke up to what was happening and expressed their own concerns, especially some of the immigrant faiths such as the Muslims and Hindus. The BCC switchboard was also jammed with angry critics of the stand the Council was taking. On the Continent there were similar late protests from national Catholic and Protestant councils, from academics, and not least from the special committee of the Dutch Parliament. This had been steadily investigating the new movements and their undoubted problems for over three years and described the Cottrell proposals as 'built on quicksand'.

All this made no difference whatsoever. On 22 May 1984 the European Parliament Assembly adopted the Cottrell proposals in the dying stages of that particular Parliament. So near the end in fact, that only 22 percent of its members attended the debate – 153 out of 567. And it was carried by 98 votes out of this 567, with 28 against, and 27 abstentions: about one sixth of the Parliament in favour. That's how some things get done in politics! Nothing of the protests and criticisms from substantial church and other bodies got through at all.

In reading the full verbatim report of the debate in the Assembly it is evident that almost nothing said or done by substantial church and other bodies had made the slightest difference. There were the same old unchecked horror stories from hysterical parents, the same bland assurances that no one's religious freedom was threatened, and that this was all in accord with European declarations on human rights. It is plain that in post-Christendom Europe, as in secular New Zealand, the churches can expect to be either ignored or snubbed. Even MEP Sir Fred Catherwood, widely known as a respected evangelical leader in Britain and abroad, failed to see the issues or heed Christian counsels, and spoke emotionally in support of the controls. How we need to equip committed Christian people in politics to know what they are doing.

The bright spot in all this is that European Parliament Resolutions have no mandatory power. They would have had to be ratified by a separate body, the Council of Ministers, and there was no chance of this. Both the Home and the Foreign Office ministers in Britain – then Mr Leon Brittan and Sir Geoffrey Howe – wrote to the British Council of Churches saying they had no intention of any such action. The further bright spots would have been the impossibility of enforcing any such controls, through the courts or otherwise, as any legal adviser to the Europarliament should have known. Or, as the forthright Glasgow MEP, Jenny Buchan, put it: "It won't make the blindest bit of difference."

Impractical controls

Now all this may seem a far cry from the situation of the churches, but just let me apply the proposals in this area for a moment. No life-long religious commitment by anyone under the age of majority? – what of baptism, confirmation, conversion – does one have to wait till the law says one is 'grown up'? Apart from age altogether, no conversion or adoption of a new faith while away from one's own country. Would a Hindu or Sikh student convert have to go back to India first? And a migrant worker or traveller must take care not to get converted while away from home.

Who are the so-called 'competent authorities' to enforce all this, and what is their competence? The police, some local bureaucrat or religious inspector? And armed with authority to demand that our own minister tell them where you or I are at any time? As if even the minister needs to know all this, much less report it. Divulging even the list of church members to another party, without the consent of each member, is specifically prohibited in the new Privacy Acts in New Zealand and elsewhere.

There were 13 clauses of this kind in the so-called 'guidelines' that would have become requirements. I shall mention only one more of this preposterous lot. Parents were to be given unrestricted access to their family, at all times, free to pressure them to leave their religious commitments, at any age – 30, 50, 60...? The American authority on religious liberty called it establishment of "perpetual religious infancy"!

The one thing some people need badly is to be able to escape from oppressive or criminal, degenerate or severely dysfunctional families. We can all think of situations like this. Across this whole debate you will find a wrong and one-sided, normative and authoritative position given to the family – and this in a society busy undermining the family in so many other ways! The thinking on this subject has been simply appalling.

The chief effects of these goings-on in Strasbourg might well have been the reinforcement they gave to harassment elsewhere, especially of the Unificationists. It was later that year, in 1984, that the British Attorney-General began his court action against them. In the October David Alton, well-known Liberal Party MP and a Catholic, explicitly sought to implement the Strasbourg Parliamentary 'guidelines' by introducing a private member's bill in the House of Commons "to control the activities of religious sects and cults".

Like most private bills it did not get far. The irony was that Mr Alton customarily spoke with passionate conviction about the rights of religious dissidents behind the Iron Curtain, and shortly afterwards wrote an article in the London *Times* protesting against persecution of Christians in the Hindu Kingdom of Nepal, and quoting the U.N. Convention on Human Rights! How divided can one's mind be?

The main lessons to be extracted from the Strasbourg story concern how politics works in religious matters, the professional incompetency of some political and legal organs in this area, the way Western culture can simply snub the Christian churches, the fragility of religious liberty and the presence of discrimination and intolerance amid all the confident talk about human rights, and by the same people.

I am a member of that remarkable voluntary body, Amnesty International. Its reports often feature success in releasing those in prison on account of their religious convictions in places like Iran or North Korea or Cuba. Shortly after the Strasbourg Resolutions, Amnesty's journal in Britain contained a feature article on the wonderful Human Rights record of the European

Parliament. This was too much for me, and I wrote a letter pointing out how this Parliament had blotted it's copybook with its recent Resolutions. But they would not publish the letter, not even Amnesty. In Iran, or Korea or Cuba? – yes; but not among ourselves – 'It couldn't happen here!'

Human rights and the Enlightenment

I will finish this story with a brief account of how I discovered something of where I stood on human rights. In 1987, amid all these events of the decade, I was invited to read a paper on 'Religious Liberty in Britain in the 20th Century' at an International Seminar on New Religious Movements and the Law, at the ancient University in the Roman city of Parma in north Italy. I prepared a more detailed account of some of the things I have mentioned here.

For a day and a half I listened to historians, sociologists, constitutional and ecclesiastical lawyers, and other disciplines relate the sorry records of Western European governments' dealings with new religious movements. Then I realised that they were all showing how government actions had breached the right to religious freedom enshrined in the written constitutions of all these states, from Scandinavia to Spain. And further, that all these written constitutions derived from the 18th century Enlightenment philosophies and especially from the French and American Revolutions late in that century. I think the Danish constitution of 1815 was the first to emerge from this background. Religious freedom and toleration were among the basic human rights.

Now all these constitutions were based on the Enlightenment's views of religion being entitled to freedom so long as it remained a matter of private opinion, so long as it makes no claims to present a public truth with authority over the nation and the state. In order to escape harassment or to secure immediate freedom of action, both new religions and the older and larger faiths may gladly and unquestionably have accepted this particular basis for their liberty.[4]

Most faiths, apart from those in tribal cultures, believe that their truth is for everybody, and not just one private opinion among many. There is therefore a hidden paradox, if not hypocrisy, in accepting this constitutional basis that we do not really believe in for the sake of the freedom offered by the state on its own terms. By this time I was sharing in the British Gospel and Our Culture project that was exposing the false assumptions of this very 18th century Enlightenment philosophy. So what was I doing here in this Catholic University in Parma, sharing in all this acceptance of a false basis for religious freedom and tolerance – this humanist view of religions as free so long as they remained private hobbies and kept out of the public sphere?

Discovering myself on human rights

It was an awkward question. I had hurriedly to add something to my thinking and to my paper before its presentation late on the second day. I said: "I reject both this view of religion and the Enlightenment philosophy from which it derives. My model for religious liberty is not found in the inherent dignity and rights of all people. In a century that is not only the Great Age of Religious Persecution but also the Great Age of Genocide, what kind of unrealistic basis is that? These rights are derivative and not inherent; and this dignity is both derivative and only potential, rather than a present achievement. My model is found not in any human and unenforceable, abstract theory of rights, but elsewhere. It is found in the way that God treats me and all people by giving us freedom to err in our theologizing and to sin in our living, and even freedom to try to get rid of him by killing him, as history testifies" [I was getting into a somewhat dramatic stride by now] "and as history testifies in the form of the crucifix hanging above the entrance doors to this meeting hall!" Remember it was a largely Catholic university, and in the great lecture room there it was, a crucifix suspended above the doors, to which I pointed with some emotion.

Then I went on: "With that ultimate sanction for religious toleration I am able to tolerate other bases among those with whom I combine for practical action in this sphere, bases I regard as inadequate or false, as I regard those emanating from the Enlightenment. Toleration therefore for me begins at home, in the community represented by this assembly, or wherever such theories are held."

Many did not know what to make of this academic turned traitor or preacher. But I know that some at least appreciated a bit of Christian truth for a change. One was the wife of the rector or vice-chancellor of a university in Paris, themselves of the Reformed Church in France. She told me it was very Calvinistic, and very British! I think I welcomed both adjectives.

But most important of all, with this bit of homespun and impromptu theology I discovered the essence of the matter for myself, on the run, as it were, and in the most unexpected of circumstances. Perhaps it takes situations like these to show us to ourselves. This time I like to think there may have been a quiet smile of satisfaction in heaven; that at last, he's got the point.

The Afrikaner Churches of South Africa:
Boycotts or Bridges?

I think my first awareness of South Africa must have been those war memorials in New Zealand towns often showing a soldier in uniform, standing complete with rifle, commemorating those who went from this country to join the British, the 'mother country', in what was called the Boer War at the turn of the 20th century. Seldom must New Zealanders have understood so little of what the issues really were.

I could not then have imagined that later in life I would find myself defending the descendants of these Boers against British and others who were fighting them, this time not with bullets but with bannings and boycotts. I cannot suggest that Providence has found any amusement in this, but surely some sense of its irony, which is next door to laughter.

South Africa has figured several times in earlier stories, in relation to independent African religious movements claiming to be Christian churches. Current estimates speak of something like 4000 identifiable movements – denominations, large or small, in our terms – with perhaps over four million members, known collectively as 'Zionists'. Earlier I spoke of how the large Zion Christian Church brought together the three main political leaders at their great church gathering at Easter in 1994. They have been among the many Christian reconciling agents in modern South Africa.

Guest of the academic world

It was my involvement in the study of movements like these that led to a most surprising invitation in 1979. It came from the committee of vice-chancellors of the 13 South African universities, with further unofficial invitations to visit another five universities in the so-called independent homelands, and also some of the separate theological seminaries. I was to lecture on these new tribally-based religious movements so prolific in Africa and elsewhere. The British Council would pay the fare – on the assumption I was an emissary of British life and culture! It was to be a demanding few months in which I managed to visit 14 universities and a number of the seminaries.

Except for two universities, Cape Town and Natal, I was in the care and in the homes of either Afrikaner or African academics or churchmen, and on the Sundays I was in their churches. Most visitors from abroad like me were hosted by the English-origin population and their churches, where one could more freely join in the world condemnation of apartheid. It seemed as though I would be in the other camp and be heavily compromised by this intimate association.

No one was known to me in South Africa. The invitation was initiated by Professor Oosthuizen, professor of religious studies at the then new university at Westville near Durban for the Indian population. I knew of his own scholarly work on these movements, but as a very theologically-minded Afrikaner he had originally adopted a critical, doctrinal attitude towards them from which I had had to dissent – at a distance. He later became and remained the chief champion of their sympathetic study.

I was accustomed to relating to these marginalized and despised movements. Now I found that I was dealing with Afrikaners who claimed to be fellow Christians, but who themselves felt marginalized and despised by the outside world.

This was not what I had expected from my visit. Looking back, I think as much if not more was done for relations with the Afrikaner churches than with the new indigenous movements on whose account I had ostensibly come to South Africa. Here were what would normally be regarded as 'mainline' churches banned and attacked by the main Christian body overseas, just like their own Zionists were, so that their story belongs in this collection along with my other stories of rejection. Here was another of those unexpected directives of Providence and I simply had to let it happen and follow through.

My arrival on a Saturday was not exactly encouraging. Upon entry at Johannesburg I innocently and too fully declared that I was visiting "to lecture in universities". So where was my work permit? Acting as a semi-VIP official visitor didn't succeed! No permit, no entry. No one had thought of this. I was held at the airport, missed my onward flight to Capetown, and waited for hours hoping something was happening. Finally my very polite captors told me they had reached the senior immigration officer by phone at home before he went off to Saturday afternoon rugby, and he would let me in for two weeks. I could apply later for extension. Strangely, when I did apply in Capetown for the extension, they couldn't care less or give it fast enough. I was not impressed with South African administration.

From re-victualling stop to settlers

Before proceeding with my own limited story I must outline some of the unique history of South Africa. You will find it well done by an outsider, in James A. Michener's 1000-page blockbuster, simply called *The Covenant*. One wishes all the boycotting opponents of apartheid had first read it; my Afrikaner friends say it is mostly accurate.

The modern history of this end of Africa begins with the establishment in 1652 of a small revictualling station at the Cape for the ships of the Dutch East Indies Company on their long haul from Europe to what is now Indonesia. The basic point is that the Cape settlement was not a European colony, only a supply stop and then a trading station. Elsewhere colonies from Europe were developing local versions of the basic European institutions – the press, universities, church systems with theological seminaries, and organs of government and the arts. The motherland maintained responsibility but fostered these developments and remained in constant communication.

None of this was happening at the Cape. The East Indies Company actually *forbade any such local development or industries or trade*. Some of the Dutch who manned it, contrary to Company policy, settled there, spread out, took up land and farmed, used Hottentots (who were not Bantu by race) for labour and imported other labour from the East Indies. Inter-marriage of all these elements produced the mixed race known now as the 'Coloureds'. For almost two centuries the growing Dutch community was on its own, cut off from European history, later even developing its own Afrikaner language from the old High Dutch. This is the first key to undersstanding the Afrikaners. They were left behind and ignored by Europe.

Broken by colonial conquest

The second key is the 19th century story of the colonization and conquest of South Africa by the British. They simply failed to understand this unique history, and tried to assimilate and update these unsophisticated, rural people who actually outnumbered the English settlers by eight to one. They suffered much misunderstanding and injustice from the British. It was imperialism's ugly face, this time towards fellow Europeans and Christians.

So the Afrikaners abandoned their farms and trekked north in search of freedom. The Great Trek of 1836 is one of the epics of history. It is a moving experience to any but the most biased to visit the great monument to it on the hilltop outside Pretoria, with its bas-reliefs telling the story of these 'Boers' and their families in the ox-wagons, driving their herds with them.

Thus it was that they encountered Zulu and other tribes who were moving south and west. In 1838 about 200 Boer trekkers were met by some 10,000 Zulu warriors. They made a covenant to keep the day as a sabbath and to build a church if God would give them the victory. With religious fervour and superior weapons they won, and the local river was renamed Blood River – from Zulu blood. And so the great annual Afrikaner celebration is 'The Day of the Covenant' – and hence the title of Michener's book. 'With God's help we will stand alone against any opposition and we will survive.' That is the self-understanding that has supported the stubborn Afrikaner against the world.

The British also moved north, and finally conquered the free republics the Boers had established. The Anglo-Boer War of 1899-1902 was the tragic result, with the inevitable British victory. It is better not to dwell on the savage British treatment of the Boers: a scorched earth policy that razed 30,000 farms and 20 villages, and the world's first modern concentration camps for their women and children – 26,000 died of disease and starvation, fellow Europeans and fellow Christians.

The Afrikaners were broken, and their language banned from the schools. The church was their only free institution, and church and people were welded together in suffering as never before. No wonder they formed a society that became ever more secret, the Broederbond, the Brotherhood, to support one another and retain a sense of their culture and identity. A fierce, thwarted nationalism developed and they identified with the suffering Israel of the Bible, which was the only book many of them had ever had.

We may pause here to note the remarkable parallel between the Afrikaners and the Rastafarians, who also relied upon one book, the King James Bible. In this book they both found the story of Israel as a small people uprooted from their homeland and taken into the exile of Babylon. The Afrikaners had escaped from the British in their 'exodus' north into the promise of their own free republics, only to find these destroyed, as literally as Jerusalem in the scorched earth policy, and as humiliatingly as the Babylonian exile in the return to colonial status. In the next chapter I shall deal with how they attempted to deal with this as an elect people accompanied by a new doctrine of apartheid.[1] The Rastafari in Jamaica had been exiled from their African homeland by the European powers, the new Babylon, and subjected to the cruellest of slavery, and then a legal emancipation that left them still humiliated, ruled by Babylon the colonial master, and no nearer their homeland. Their response was to identify with Israel , especially with the Psalms that sang their trust in Jah while they awaited the downfall of Babylon. The story of Israel has so readily become the story of oppressed peoples, whether in the Caribbean, in South Africa or across the world.

Recovery by apartheid

I must skip the survival and recovery story of the next 40 years, until in 1948 by sheer numbers at the polling booths they voted in an Afrikaner government, and so began the South Africa of the next four decades, the apartheid period which is all that most of us know. It takes an appreciation of their own long oppression and struggle for survival against both Black Africans and white British to understand this deliberate policy of strict separation of the races on the part of a deeply Christian people.

It is common to explain this combination of apartheid and Christianity in terms of the stereotyped 'rigid Calvinism' of Afrikaner religion. It was Calvin's doctrine of predestination that allegedly explained the Afrikaner sense of being a people chosen or predestined for survival and, like ancient Israel, to remain distinct among the nations. This is simply not true. Calvin had no doctrine of predestination of nations or peoples – only of individuals.

And in any case until the 20th century hardly any Afrikaners or their home-grown untheological ministers had ever heard of Calvin. This is a convenient Western libel both of Calvin and of the Afrikaners.

While this Calvinism was supposed to be at work, the great Dutch neo-Calvinist in Holland of the turn of the century, Abraham Kuyper, was declaring that human advance depended upon "the commingling of blood" and that the most advanced nations, who were Calvinist like Holland, exhibit this "mingling of races". No basis for apartheid there! How perversely wrong the stereotyped history in the public mind can be.

Nor was it apartheid in the modern sense that had first led to the establishment of separate Black and Coloured sections of the Afrikaner churches. In the earlier Boer centuries all those living on the farm worshipped together, white farmers and Black workers. It was only later in the 19th century as mission work developed among the Black tribes that separate churches were set up, not for racial reasons, but for greater missionary effectiveness through use of the various vernaculars and customs.

In fact the origins of modern apartheid are quite complex and quite late – mostly after the defeat in the Anglo-Boer War. Put briefly, there was a distorted reversal of Kuyper's teaching, especially in the smallest of the three Afrikaner churches, with its university at Potschefstroom, and for reasons that can be traced. This combined with the influence from the 1920s of the Nazi revival of Germany from her defeat in World War I and her shameful humiliation at the hands of the victors through the Treaty of Versailles. Afrikaner students went to Germany for graduate study and the parallel was inevitable: Aryan survival by purity of race; Afrikaner survival likewise.

Nothing of Calvin in all this! The later theological critique of apartheid drew heavily upon the discovery by young Afrikaner theologians from the 1960s, of the theology of the great Karl Barth, who stood within the Calvinist tradition. How back-to-front popular journalism and history can be! This background is necessary to understand my own more prosaic story; I hope it will prevent any impression that I was soft on apartheid itself.

The Nico Smith story

After overcoming the entrance hurdle there began a simply wonderful two months or so, in the hands of some of the most impressive and hospitable people I have ever met. I began at Stellenbosch, the second oldest town, founded three centuries earlier in 1679, and with its university regarded as the Oxford of South Africa.

I was in the home of Nico Smith, professor of missiology and religions, in the university theological faculty-cum-seminary of the Dutch Reformed Church. His wife, Ellen, was lecturing in psychiatry in the medical school in Capetown. A handsome and charming pair in a lovely Dutch colonial-style house in this beautiful university town surrounded by vineyards; for a visitor – idyllic.

His story can be sketched, partly from his own conversation and partly from the book since written about him: *Outside the Gate*, by Rebecca de Saintonge (1989). He turned out to be one of the most dramatic figures in the struggle against apartheid within the Dutch Reformed Church – the 'DRC'. Strangely, before I left South Africa I was to be the guest of his opposite number, the leader of the later fanatical and doomed plan to move out and form a small all-white secessionist state within the new multi-racial South Africa. This was Carel Boshoff, also a professor of missiology and religions, in the University of Pretoria; when he was a student he was one of Nico Smith's closest friends! There you have epitomised the painful polarised struggle over apartheid within the main Afrikaner church, the DRC.

Here I can offer only the briefest of sketches of Nico Smith's life. His mother had been a child of about seven in one of the concentration camps. She had watched her own grandmother die there. Her father's farm had been reduced to rubble. Nico grew up hating the British – no English was ever spoken in his home. He shared in the euphoria in 1948 when the Afrikaners won the general election. He trained for the ministry, as an able, devout, evangelistically enthusiastic young Afrikaner.

After a year or so as assistant in prosperous town churches he felt a call as a missionary to the still largely non-Christian rural Black population. Although apartheid policies were taking shape there was no contradiction in this for him. So in 1956 Nico and Ellen, his doctor wife, and their baby pioneered a new mission station in the remote north among the Venda tribe. With their own hands they built their house and a mission hospital and established a congregation of 400.

This is but one example of the notable mission work of the Afrikaners among the Black Africans that has led to large Black Churches parallel to the white ones, and for which they are given no credit in the outside world. Yes, 'parallel' and apart, but still churches.

Apartheid, however, still ruled Nico Smith's thinking. He told me how he'd been invited during this time to an all-day ecumenical meeting with black and white clergy of various churches besides those of the Afrikaners. At lunchtime he found they were to be sitting down together and he knew he couldn't do that; but the hostess said: "Don't worry, Mr Smith; I've laid a place for you in my husband's study." So Nico self-righteously ate alone.

After seven years as a missionary he was invited to become missions administrator for his church in the northern Transvaal. He accepted if he could first have three months in Europe to discover the missions thinking going on there. And he wanted to meet Karl Barth, who he had heard was the 'greatest theologian in the world'.

In 1963 he did just this. Barth asked him some searching questions about how free he was to preach the Gospel if he found this differed from his own church's teaching. Barth said he'd been reading Prime Minister H.F. Vervoerd's statements on race, which sounded just like those in the southern USA before the American Civil War! Was South Africa a hundred years behind the times? Which I have already suggested *was* where the Afrikaners had been in their own history.

In and out of the Broederbond

Barth had led the opposition to the Nazi German theories that had been so influential in South Africa. Nico Smith was now confused by this man he admired so much theologically, but he was still unconvinced. Publicly he was so identified with apartheid that he was invited, after the usual close investigation, to join the select and secret society of the Broederbond, with its mysterious rituals and vows to work for the Afrikaner nation.

This privileged membership soon changed the course of his life. After three years as a missions administrator, in 1966 he was pressed by the Broederbond to apply for a vacant lectureship in missiology at the prestigious Stellenbosch University. This was to keep out a much better qualified applicant, with whom we were later to stay, David Bosch, who was not a Broederbonder. Nico knew he wasn't ready, but one doesn't oppose the Broederbond. So he got the lectureship. Although doubts were emerging and Ellen was pressing him to resign from the Broederbond, he knew he'd never get promotion to the chair in missiology that was coming up if he did so; and in due course he got it.

His first eight years at Stellenbosch were a period of spiritual searching and mental trauma. Then in 1973 all members of the Broederbond were called upon to re-affirm their vows in view of a breakaway of extreme rightists that had occurred. Nico found he couldn't, and resigned. But it was more than the Broederbond from which he was resigning; it was a public departure from the whole ruling philosophy and theology of apartheid.

Six years later, when I was staying with him, he told me of what he went through in these years from colleagues and his own students, and from the university administration and the Broederbond-dominated theological faculty. He had been reprimanded by the Rector (or vice-chancellor) on trumped-up charges, threatened by the faculty, ostracized with his wife socially, and had his phone tapped by the police. One of his students came and confessed that he could no longer continue as a police informer in his classes.

His teaching of course was profoundly altered through his changed position, and some of his students were responding positively. A few came one night to his house to support him. He told me he wept. The climax was to come just over two years later.

Blacks from the so-called separate homelands states had been flooding into the Republic looking for work. Many had set up in a squatter camp outside Capetown. In desperate attempts to stem the flow the government had been bulldozing the shanties and putting their occupants on buses back to the homelands; but they just returned again.

Nico decided to take some of his so-comfortably-brought-up students to see the camp. It rocked most of them. They were to talk about it in the next lecture; but a few were Broederbond informers and reported to the faculty Dean. Before the lecture Nico was summoned and told not to discuss the camp with his students, or take them on such field-work, or make any public statements.

White minister in a Black township
Shortly afterwards there appeared a book of 24 essays called *Storm-Kompass*, critical of both apartheid and the Broederbond. Nico Smith was one of the three editors. The press had a field day with it. He was called before the

faculty yet again and knew he had come to the point of decision. He didn't sleep much that night. He couldn't continue like this. But what to do?

Next afternoon the postman came with a telegram. He opened it at once: 'You are called to the congregation of Mamelodi, Pretoria'. He burst into tears, with the postman staring at him, thinking it must be very bad news. Nico knew at once that this was the answer. But (wait for it) – Mamelodi was no affluent suburb in the beautiful capital city of Pretoria. It was a dusty black township several kilometres away, where no whites were allowed to live; yet they had dared to call him as co-pastor with the Black minister of their congregation of the Black DRC, even if he would have to live in Pretoria. Ellen left her white medical school position and got a job in a Black teaching hospital 50 kilometres away. The nearest parallel I can think of is one of the professors in a theological department being called to be the junior minister of a Maori congregation in the Hokianga, or a Black congregation in Handsworth, Birmingham.

So for two years from 1982 Nico Smith commuted daily to this Black township parish. I met him again in 1984 in Pretoria and he seemed a very tired man. Soon after this they decided they'd have to live in Mamelodi itself, but they would try to do so legally. So they wrote asking for official permission from the Minister for Native Affairs. Nine months later they got an answer, and surprisingly it was Yes. So then, where to live?

They decided to build a little round two-floored house modelled on the round African hut, and into this surprising structure they moved in 1985; as far as they know, the first whites to live in a Black township in modern times. Later that year Mamelodi was virtually taken over by militant, vigilante youth gangs with horrifying violence of Black against Black.

I can't detail the continuing story, but will give two samples. The first is of Nico being called by a youth to a group about to 'necklace' an alleged police informer – ram a tyre over his shoulders, pour petrol into it and then ignite it. Nico doesn't know how he managed to walk into that violent circle and prevent another necklacing.

The second is of the bold plan for white and Black Christians to go and live in each others' homes for a week. In 1988 over 170 whites were accommodated in Mamelodi homes one week, and some 35 Blacks spent another week in white homes – in their guest rooms, not in the servants' quarters in the backyard.

Johan Heyns, martyr

The Nico Smith story has continued in this revolutionary Christian mode. It indicates the struggle against apartheid within the Afrikaner churches. And while this was a dramatic and public example there were many others who had opposed apartheid from the political beginnings back in the 1940s. Even then the world knew of Alan Paton and read his *Cry the Beloved Country*. But he wasn't an Afrikaner, and it was the Afrikaners who had introduced apartheid who had to undo it. And above all the Dutch Reformed Church; in the 1980s some 80 percent of the cabinet and 70 percent of all MPs were members of the DRC. Church and state were intertwined.

There were many who were trying from within the church. I could list the leading theological professors and churchmen who were tried for 'heresy' or expelled – such as Beyers Naudé whom I met while he was under government house arrest. And there was a series of tentative manifestos and theological critiques of apartheid. As early as the 1950s a DRC commission was recognising "race relations that possibly do not accord with the Word of God." By 1974 it was admitting that there was "no Scriptural foundation" for apartheid – in a church that takes the Bible very seriously. By 1982 it was declaring that the policy had to be "completely revised in the light of Scripture". None of this was reported by the Western press or picked up by white visitors, and those working from the inside to secure these steps felt deserted by their fellow Christians overseas.

In 1986 it elected an openly reforming moderator of Synod for four years, Johan Heyns, a theology professor in Pretoria. The General Synod that year made the revolutionary statements that the church was fully open to all races, and actually confessed that apartheid had been a sin! He was interviewed on TV in Britain, shown between 11.50 pm and 10 minutes past midnight. That's how the most significant news often gets treated.

He told how he had first discovered his Christian equality with Blacks when as a young man he was on doctoral studies in Holland. In the Reformed churches their communicants go forward in relays and sit together on benches around the long communion table to receive the elements. And he had found himself sitting at the Lord's table beside a Black! He had to wait for some three decades to see this relationship accepted officially in his own church under his moderatorship.

He also appealed for what he called 'critical solidarity' with his church on the part of the Christians in Britain, who were still busy banning and boycotting. I had earlier met him at Pretoria University, so I wrote appreciating the TV interview and answering the appeal for solidarity.

I also accepted the invitation to make it '*critical* solidarity'. I suggested that world opinion might well be shifted from the economic sanctions issue to the more specific question of police treatment of those under arrest or in prison. The Steve Biko story and others are very upsetting and seemed to me intolerable in a civilized and Christian country. I told him that when I discussed this with Afrikaner friends there did not seem to be a very clear response. I had been told that the police were poorly paid, little educated, and too few in number; there were in fact three times as many police in Britain in proportion to the population as in South Africa. All these were valid explanations, but equally they were valid points for reform. Professor Heyns replied appreciating the solidarity and accepting the criticism.

So while Nico Smith worked up front, people like Johan Heyns were working within and through the church system. It was these people who had to pass the Synod declarations and deal with all the misunderstandings, fears and prejudices within the congregations. I don't know how some of them did it.

I don't know the ongoing price some may yet have to pay, as they live with the hatreds they aroused from some of their own kind. For late in 1994, right on the heels of the ending of apartheid, Johan Heyns was assassinated – shot through a window when sitting in his own house in a Pretoria suburb, and almost certainly by a white.[2] Truly a bitter qualification of the euphoria around the world in that year. I know of many martyrs in the cause of equality in South Africa, but I should think he is the first prominent white churchman to have been murdered on this account. This belated revenge is an inverted tribute to his contribution and an indication of the problems that remain.

In the homes of both parties

On my second visit in 1984 I went with Maude, to address the South Africa Missiological Society Annual conference and to have the seaside holiday I mentioned in the previous story. In a lush Pretoria suburban DRC church we spent a Sunday with Dr. Piet Meiring, the minister. My address encouraged the congregation to take African independent churches, their rather despised Zionists, more seriously. But while Piet Meiring was a radical reformer his congregation then included the leader of the breakaway extreme right Conservative party – Dr André Treurnicht. Somehow Piet Meiring both held such a congregation together, and worked publicly for reform.

That Sunday afternoon as we talked in the manse Meiring was called to the phone. The Minister of Broadcasting had just banned transmission that evening of a TV programme when he heard that Dr Meiring was to be on the panel to be interviewed. It was the sort of thing that harassed and frustrated those working within the Afrikaner and other churches against apartheid.

I would like to tell of the three weeks Maude and I spent as guests in the home of the greatest South African I have known, David Bosch, and his wife Annemie. He was the one the Broederbond had used Nico Smith to keep out of Stellenbosch; and now they were in the same team, Nico at Mamelodi and David Bosch in Pretoria as dean of one of the largest theological faculties in the world, in the huge distance University of South Africa. This has no students on campus but some hundred thousand all over the world.

David Bosch kindly arranged a short visiting fellowship in the university to help us pay the fare. I hope I justified it in seminars with the faculty. So I shared in his work style. At 6 am we rose for breakfast, together with his eight-year-old son who was going deaf after an accident. At 6.30 we left home, dropped the boy off at a pick-up point for a bus collecting deaf children for a special school, and by 7 am we were in our offices at the university for a 10-hour day. Then home for him to work in the evenings on his major study on mission theory, *Transforming Mission*. It is already used as a classic all over the world.

Both David Bosch and his wife Annemie were *persona non grata* in their own congregation but beloved by Blacks and reforming whites elsewhere. I think of him as the outstanding missiologist of our time, who died after a tragic motor accident in 1992. Yet he did live to see his *magnum opus* published in 1991, and to see the beginnings of the revolution of the 1990s. I hope that was enough.

As I have stressed, this revolution had been gathering pace for much longer than outside people realised. Even a visitor like myself could see definite changes back between 1979 and 1984. Blacks no longer left the pavement and walked past in the gutter before oncoming whites.

One incident summed it up for me. I was in a queue for stamps in a post office in a small town; in front of me was a white woman, smoking a cigarette; when she had finished with it she leaned around past me and pushed the butt into the hand of an African woman immediately behind me, with a motion indicating to go and put it in the ash-bucket by the wall. And the African woman just did it. I was pretty horrified – until I realised that five years earlier that could not have happened, because *there would have been two separate queues*. So it is two steps forward and one back, as in so much social progress.

There were of course the die-hards. Earlier I had been the house guest of the leader of the rump of the Broederbond – for it had been broken through the changes – Professor Carel Boshoff, on his farm just outside Pretoria. I mentioned him above as the leader of the white secession movement and as a polar opposite to Nico Smith.

His wife Ann's father was the chief architect of apartheid from the 1950s, Dr. Verwoerd. When he was Prime Minister in 1966 he was assassinated by a white man within the Parliament buildings. His daughter was a somewhat formidable and formal but still gracious hostess, and helped me in further awkward plans I had to make. I don't think we discussed politics very much.

One could talk, even if fruitlessly, with her gentle bear of a husband, Carel; and he was a best friend of Nico Smith in their student days. Even then, in 1979, he and his wife and leaders in the Broederbond were publicly admitting that apartheid had failed. The outside world didn't hear this astonishing confession for what it was.

On another occasion I was the guest for three days of the Rev. J.L. Strijdom, a scholarly DRC minister who had recently been principal of the Sebokeng Interdenominational Theological State Training College during its seven years' existence – which means a government seminary for the leaders of the independent or Zionist churches. In New Zealand that would translate as a government theological college especially to train ministers for the Ratana and Ringatu religions. Quite unbelievable!

This is a fascinating and unknown story: why it began in good faith, taking these despised bodies seriously, if somewhat naively and paternal-istically, what it taught, and why it failed. But it remains as an example of the missionary outreach of the DRC, and of the government attempts to deal positively with Black Africans in the midst of the apartheid era.

So those on the now losing side were not simply evil, unchristian people.

I could not say that of my hosts, the Boshoffs or the Strijdoms, as over against the Boschs and the Nico Smiths.

Banning and boycotting, or bridge-building?

While the changes I have outlined were occurring in the largest Afrikaner church there were corresponding political changes. First in the mid-1980s through the new president, P.W. Botha, and we began to hope much from him. Even Bishop Desmond Tutu speculated that he could prove to be South Africa's greatest political leader, although in the end he was a great disappointment. But the Africa Secretary in the British Council of Churches wrote to me in 1984, unwilling to recognise any signs of change: "P.W. Botha has a cunning that will cause history to evaluate him as the most dangerously evil leader apartheid has known." How blind one can be; but my correspondent was an English South African in exile, and they often understood least and had some reason for bitterness.

Many like him were prophesying bloody revolution, and declaring that it was 'one minute to midnight', if not already five minutes past. I hope they haven't felt let down by the suddenness, speed and comparative smoothness of the transition. They just hadn't seen what was really happening; they tended to dismiss all changes as 'merely cosmetic'. Although Botha disappointed us, his successor F.W. de Klerk proved the Afrikaner for the hour; and of course there was Nelson Mandela to match him and work with him.

A question in retrospect is how far the international boycott policies contributed to the ending of apartheid. My own feeling is (apart from the sports boycott that I supported) – much less than people would like to think. I for one as a Christian was in the bridge-building business, not the banning and boycotting. Mrs. Thatcher was a lone voice in the Commonwealth leaders' conferences, refusing to go along with general economic boycotting. I found it a little uncomfortable to be agreeing with her. In any case I totally opposed the Church and university boycotts operating in Britain.

Some experiences of South Africa by other Christians were in effect unwitting boycotts. While we were staying with the Boschs, a young English United Reformed Church ordinand connected with our own congregation in Birmingham came for six months' experience in a congregation of the white Presbyterian Church of South Africa in a Pretoria suburb. If we hadn't asked him over to meet David and Annemie Bosch he would have returned to Britain without ever talking with an Afrikaner church minister in the same Reformed tradition.

The tendency in Britain and elsewhere, naturally enough, was to listen to the Black Christian leaders like the Anglican Bishop Desmond Tutu and Dr. Allan Boesak, the Coloured DRC minister who has since been disgraced and imprisoned. I often found their public pronouncements too strident and abrasive. Of course they had been adopted by the media because of their stridency and given prime time, while Afrikaner Johan Heyns in the very centre of the struggle was relegated to midnight.

I felt they were not free men. On the one hand, to get a hearing, they had to fill the roles forced on them by the outside Christian world, and to denounce apartheid and the government in other people's virulent terms. And within South Africa they were competing for Black support with the violent and often Marxist voices from the large African political organizations that then had no Nelson Mandela up front. I sometimes found their statements embarrassing, but perhaps I was asking too much of them.

As an Anglican, Desmond Tutu was not in a major South African church, although it was an expatriate Anglican, Trevor Huddleston, who so powerfully brought apartheid to world Christian attention in his book *Naught For Your Comfort* of a generation previously. But Huddleston was banned from entry and became increasingly out of date. This had a distorting effect when he led the British anti-apartheid movement, now with archbishop's status – 'of the Indian Ocean'!

Against the stream in Britain

I had occasion to raise this at the Selly Oak Colleges in Birmingham after he became Provost or titular head of the Colleges' Federation. He returned from a tour of the states surrounding South Africa and gave a public lecture at Selly Oak. I had not long returned myself from being inside the Afrikaner community. My own minister was at the meeting and knew what I thought about the changing situation and about boycotting, which was Huddleston's method. I knew my minister would rate me as a coward if I said nothing to qualify Huddleston's account. So I ventured to swim against the emotional tide of the meeting and add some other information of my own inside gathering. But who was I to question this famous Archbishop? I doubt if I was heard.

In the 1980s the British universities were also being admonished to boycott South African academics. Birmingham University refused to accept research scholars who wanted to come there when it learned they were funded by South African government grants. The staff Bulletin printed a long justification of this; as technically a staff member (I held an honorary research fellowship) I wrote a critique of this, but the Bulletin refused to publish it.

The academics in South Africa, whether Afrikaner or Anglophone, and especially those opposed to apartheid, felt this pariah treatment keenly; this was one reason why I received an unduly warm welcome. They were almost pathetically grateful to anyone who accepted them as fellow Christians and tried to support them in their own struggles against apartheid. A non-Afrikaner from Natal University actually wrote an article in the British *Guardian* newspaper criticizing the professor of theology in Birmingham for her boycott position. What he wanted was international, and especially Christian, contact and support.

My Birmingham minister had written to a South African friend and mentioned myself as a New Zealander interested in his country. He wrote back with a story of how he had been walking on the Mount of Beatitudes by the Sea of Galilee, when he entered into conversation with two New Zealanders. When they recognised his accent they said: "We do not speak to South Africans", and turned their backs on him.

South Africa rejoins the world

We all have much to atone for. But the door is now open wide for a new relationship with Christians of all kinds in South Africa. These people have known churches where ministers are thoroughly trained, where they are respected and still have authority, where theology and the Bible are taken seriously, where cross-cultural missions are still a major commitment, where church attendance remains high, and family religion is impressive. They are in for a shock when they discover the situation in many of the churches in the English-speaking world.

Perhaps we need them more than they need us? They may provide a reservoir of substantial, orthodox Christianity, even if a little old-world and conservative, and not yet fully challenged by the acids of post-modernity. It is time for many of us to shed our ignorance of their unique history, and some of the self-righteousness in our past attitudes to their churches, and towards people who come from conflicts and decisions which we have been spared.

For in South Africa and across the Western societies, the very Gospel itself is being marginalized and despised, and the churches must prepare to be persecuted, as were the rejected, despised movements I have told of in these seven stories. That is one very possible scenario for societies within a Western culture that is both secular and pagan yet inheritor of the legacy of Christendom, pluralist and yet intolerantly post-modern. Forerunners of all this can be identified already in our midst.

Might it be in the good plans of Providence that others are now to be strengthened by new relations with the Afrikaner churches? The confidence represented by their own Day of the Covenant may yet assist other churches to stand firm within the Gospel Covenant against whatever tribulations lie ahead. And their great respect for the Scriptures may serve likewise to correct others' aberrations from the Gospel, just as it did, in the end, for them.

That there are great tribulations ahead of South Africa and its churches is evidenced in the problems that have emerged in the post-apartheid era. It may be that their own experience of rejection is now enabling the mainline churches to relate to the persecuted 'Zionists' in their millions in a common approach to these new problems. There has been a great deal of study of the Zionists and of joint conferencing with their leaders, promoted or supported by the Afrikaner churches and their scholars, some of whose work goes back to the 1960s. When I published my bibliography on the South African movements in 1977 there were very few authors from the Afrikaner churches in the 347 items collected; now the situation would be reversed.

Among the few pioneers in this rapprochement was anthropologist Berthold Pauw (1960s-70s); another was Danie van Zyl working with the Council of Churches for better training of Zionist ministers (from the 1960s); others have been mentioned above – Beyers Naudé, David Bosch, G.C. ('Pippin') Oosthuizen (who changed from opponent to supporter), to whom must be added Hennie Pretorius who has laboured on this mission for nearly 30 years. Many others not known personally to me have emerged in the 1990s and the future looks bright for a united approach from this so variegated Christian community to its country's problems. Life on the margins for both kinds of persecuted or rejected Christian communities will be a thing of the past.

What These Stories Say To Us

Personal stories, emerging from a diary or from reflections upon one's past, are a popular genre in our Western culture. It is part of the emphasis upon the individual and the local as against the corporate, the institutional and the traditional. It has been especially evident in the feminist movement where women are encouraged to tell their own stories no matter how humble the domestic level, to help to correct the predominance of men in conventional history. As we all become units in a mass society, there is a renewed interest in genealogy and family history with its personal recollections and stories of our forebears. Likewise, even in a discipline such as theology, some of my readers will recognize the term 'narrative theology' as a recognized mode for theological expression. This is the cultural background in which I have to offer my seven stories.

More than autobiography

While these stories are largely autobiographical, they cannot be reduced to that category and explained in terms of the idiosyncracies and curiosity of a brash, uninhibited New Zealander that land him among the odd, the outcast and the oppressed. At the same time I believe there is something in this origin and upbringing that frees from the crippling aspect of traditions and from too great a concern for the respectable and the institutional. From the opposite side of the world I and my fellow New Zealanders may appear as brash, but this cultural inheritance may well have led me in directions that others have hesitated to explore.

This freedom may also have led me to a life largely outside organized church structures and into some strange places. However, the early establishment of a neo-orthodox and 'square' personal theology in the classical tradition has proved adequate to include later mainline developments. This has also enabled me to learn from some of these movements (Moral Rearmament, the Africans and the Afrikaners), without being threatened by any of them, and without drifting into a soft theological liberalism in order to relate to them.

In telling these stories I claim therefore no personal virtues of insight, tolerance, or missionary initiative. As I have repeatedly asserted, these stories occurred in their unexpected ways simply because they were waiting to happen and, assisted by my culture, I allowed them to do so. If that is a virtue then I cannot disclaim it; but it leaves me in a very minor role as they unfold.

The common thread: unacknowledged Western persecution

Each of these stories stands alone. There is, however, a common thread running through them – that of harassment to the point of persecution of small, marginal, unorthodox, or politically incorrect religious bodies on the part of both secular governments and mainline churches *in Western societies.* To examine this more closely is part of the answer to the 'So what?' question that arises when all my stories have been told. Are they indicative of further issues in church or society?

In the later 1990s two major authoritative and detailed books (which I shall not name here) were published with the story of religious persecution and martyrdoms occurring in the *non-Western world.* The victims were usually but by no means entirely Christians, and both books supported the unwelcome statement that the 20th century has been the great century of religious persecution.

Both books, however, recounted persecutions *outside the Western world.* The scenario was therefore of an *'us and them'* nature, where the villains were *non-Westerners* and mostly non-Christians, and the implication was that we in the West could be thankful that we had progressed to religious tolerance in a religiously plural society. While these two books complemented my stories by telling of what 'they' did in the rest of the world, the books' implicit assumptions about 'us' were contradicted by my own direct experience of Western intolerance, by my stories involving religious persecutions *by Westerners*.

Another personal story

One author was on the staff of a Christian academic institution dealing especially with many of my own interests in the critique of Western culture, and with which I kept in touch through its house journal, and in other ways. I felt that the author of such a skilful book could well be encouraged to consider another parallel book, this time covering Western societies. Beyond telling my own limited experience in these seven stories I did not feel competent or free to undertake such a substantial task. I have, however, considerable documentary material on other major persecutions *within the West by Westerners* and especially in the Antipodes, but outside my direct experience. These other stories are not my own, but they badly need to be told.

I had once heard the author concerned lecturing, had read subsequent articles on the theme, and now the book. I decided therefore to raise the possibility of this author considering the task, for I was confident that there was the necessary interest and ability. I decided to send a sampling of the special documentation I had about events in the Antipodes, accompanied by a cassette tape where I could talk at length about the project and describe and offer the considerable resources I could supply. It was quite a bundle of materials.

There was not so much as an acknowledgement of our shared interests and the trouble I had taken. It then happened that a close friend of mine was to visit others in this institution who were friends of his, so I told him about the lack of response and asked him if possible to verify that my packet had arrived. He therefore made it his business to meet the staff member concerned and inquire directly. The disinterested answer was that yes it had arrived, but also that there was no intention to work through it or do anything about it. It was simply to be ignored.

Here I tell this further story because it happened to me, and because it suggests a refusal to acknowledge that what has happened in the West is in the same category and even more important than the persecutions occurring in other parts of the world. The West simply does not want to know, and some comment on this is part of the answer to the 'So what?' question of what is the point of gathering these persecutory stories together.

Stories yet to come

The stories I have told contained only minor examples of this persecutory complex, and have only touched on the resort to violence, as in the kidnapping and forcible de-programming that marked the anti-cult organizations in the 1970s and 80s of the 20th century. The most damning examples of the intolerance, injustice and violence are found in the actions of governments in Western secular societies claiming religious freedom and pluralism. Again, my stories have recorded only the milder examples, and the book for which I tried to find an author would include much more serious and tragic cases.

It might well begin with a thorough exposure of the United States government sending in tanks to destroy the Branch Davidian community in Texas in 1993, although this has essentially been done in a definitive article by Dean Kelley, the American churches' long-time specialist on religious freedom.[1]

In Australia the most notorious case of recent years would be that of Lindy Chamberlain. In 1980 she received a life sentence for the murder of her nine-week old baby at Ayer's Rock while on holiday, but was released as innocent after serving nearly three years in prison. Her treatment by the police, the justice system and the media issued in a national hysteria, and has given rise to a large amount of academic literature critiquing the whole affair. This would not seem to fall within our agenda, but I am satisfied that the way she was charged and sentenced would not have happened if she had been a member of a powerful denomination in Australia, such as the Anglicans or the Roman Catholics.[2] She was the wife of a Seventh Day Adventist pastor. This minority and socially rather despised church did not feel strong enough to rise to her defence, not even when the media claimed that the mother was carrying out a ritual of child sacrifice practised by the Adventists![3]

In my Rastafarian story I have already indicated some of the oblique ways in which injustice towards new religious movements can occur in New

Zealand, and especially the capacity of secular governments to over-react in this area. This could be developed further from the deportation of Te Kooti without trial to the Chatham Islands in 1866 that led to the Ringatu religion; through the mustering of some 2500 led by Bryce, the native Minister on a white charger, to arrest the prophets Te Whiti and Tohu in the village of Parihaka in 1881; to the force of some 70 police led by the Commissioner himself that rode in to the remote Maungapohatu utopian settlement to arrest prophet Rua (illegally, it being a Sunday) in 1916; to the Armed Offenders' Squad I have described in its ineffectual descent upon Christopher Campbell in 1986.

These were blunders against Maori, but the two most recent and serious cases of outright persecution were against whites. The first was the destructive police attack in 1977 on the Christian commune, the Full Gospel Mission at Waipara in north Canterbury, as a result of a hysterical belief in the Ministry of Defence and the Air Force that armed sedition was being planned. When tested at law, charges against the leader were dismissed in the magistrate's court.[4]

The second was the persecution of the Exclusive Brethren in Nelson by the reputable Christchurch daily, *The Press*, between 1983-85. The apparent suicide of a former member was persistently and wrongly blamed on the Brethren, of whom five individuals successfully brought defamation charges against *The Press*. Four out of five of these were upheld when the latter went to the Appeal Court – the deliverances of the various judges contain splendid statements on religious freedom.[5] It must have cost *The Press* half a million dollars. Notwithstanding, in 1995 the local Member of Parliament, Dr Nick Smith, used public occasions and parliamentary privilege to make general attacks on these same Exclusive Brethren, with full media publicity. He rejected my protest when I wrote to him, but I have been told that he had to make a 'settlement' with the Brethren.

It is plain that secular governments and public figures in New Zealand have difficulty in dealing with unfamiliar religions, but also that there has been an improvement in the protection that the courts now give to unpopular or new religious movements, even against governments and the media.

Why does a secular society bother to harass religion?

The public assumption in most Western societies, and above all in my own country, is that the public arena is empty of all dealings with religion; it is therefore neutral towards all faiths, objective and rational in its discussions, and secular and 'scientific' in its rejection of any reference to religion. Many of its élites, intellectuals and academics, however, go further than this by still accepting two standard sociological doctrines of the first half of the 20th century. These declare that whatever positive social role religion had played in the past, it was now a private and entirely personal matter, to be tolerated in its plurality of forms on the margins of society, and that if left alone there in an educated and scientific world it would gradually die out all together. So why let it bother us?

The facts of the 20th century have completely destroyed this thesis, as some sociologists have recognized for several decades. History has moved in exactly the opposite direction from that predicted.[6] This amazing century has been the great century of religious innovation with the appearance of hosts of new religions and 'sects and cults', including those I have met in my stories. It has also been the great century of revivals of earlier pagan and tribal religions and gnosticisms, as well as the great century of religious expansion, when Christianity has experienced its greatest growth ever and Asian faiths have moved anew into the wider world as migrants and missionaries.

My stories are part of the evidence that this has also been the great century for religious persecution, with more harassment and martyrs than in any single previous century. And yet these stories are of *persecutions by Westerners in Western secular societies*, where religion is not supposed to matter any more. Why, therefore, get so uptight about it? Why pursue even the smallest most inconsequential groups of new believers who have gone their often weird ways, but have broken no laws and have merely sought their own place in a confessedly plural society?

True, some have aggressively propagated their beliefs and been a nuisance at times, as the noisy Salvation Army bands were for some on a quiet Sunday morning in my home town 80 years ago. We have learned to deal with more serious practices like child abuse in our own established religious bodies, or religiously-sanctioned widow-burning, female circumcision and Qur'anic punishments coming from other faiths. We can do so again if any new movements really do have practices that cannot be tolerated in a modern society, and that are not the creations of rumour. Since this is hardly ever the case, why indiscriminately deny visas and trading permits to a class of 'new religious movements', prevent them from hiring halls, bring unsustainable charges against them like those of the British Attorney-General, secure unjust verdicts through trials by prejudiced juries as in the USA, and concoct impractical controls like those of the European Parliament?

In sum, the question is why societies that are increasingly secular in public, and profess tolerance and religious pluralism for private minorities, cannot deal with the persistence of religion, and the vitality expressed in religious innovation, especially where I have met it in minorities on 'the margins'.[7] The same questions extend beyond my own experience and into movements by no means on the margins and where religion only in the broadest sense is involved, as with the current attempts to deny public facilities to The Boy Scouts of America.

Christendom: the three worldviews on the sacred and the secular

The basic answer is that society and religion cannot do without each other – that the secular and the sacred are correlative terms, like father and son, where each defines the other. This is revealed in the language of secularism when it defines itself: it is a form of *un-belief*, or of *a-gnosticism* (without knowledge on these matters), or of *a-theism* (no god). When I was in the Department of Religious Studies in the University of Aberdeen we had a specialist, Dr. James Thrower, who produced important studies on *ir-religion*, which belonged to this department of *religion* more than to any other. In a sense, secularism is always parasitical or dependent on religion, rather than a self-defining, independent philosophy or worldview.

If this is the nature of things, then we can examine the various attempts in history to relate the two, the sacred and secular. There are really only three basic ways of doing this, represented by the three worldviews or cosmologies that I have set out in my *The Roots of Science: An Investigative Journey through the World's Religions*, and its charts.

The unitive or 'encapsulated' position of the tribal cultures, where the sacred and the secular are inseparably intertwined in one closed universe.

The dualistic view of classical Greek philosophy and most Asian religions where, in a change of terminology, the *spiritual* is distinguished and in the end separated from the *material*, as the rational and eternal reality from this irrational and ephemeral world.

The duality view of Hebrew and successor cultures where the distinction takes another form again, between a personal, good and rational *Creator* who is distinguished but never separated from the good and rationally designed *creation* that has been totally made, 'out of nothing'.

European history, like all history, begins in the tribal world and continues within the first or unitive cosmology up to the rich variety of divinities in Greek popular religion and the public religion of the Roman emperor cult. Then came the conversion of Europe to Christianity, in geographical stages and various depths, to produce the thousand years of Christendom. This was dogged on the one hand by the new dualism of Greek philosophy, fought by the early Christian thinkers, and re-introduced on the back of the Arab invasions, separating the spiritual and the material. On the other hand there was reversion to the pre-Christian tribal integration or encapsulation of the sacred in the secular. The great Christendom attempt established no new basis or formula for the relation between the sacred and the secular. Christianity had mostly replaced the tribal faiths in a similar integration with the culture, however much it changed that culture. The religion-culture principle was the same.

Secular society attempting a philosophy

Experts will shudder at this simple summarizing, but it is the essence of what happened. It is only with the gradual collapse of the integration known as Christendom, especially since the 16th century emergence of modern science and then the Enlightenment of the 18th century, that a secular Western society has emerged. For this there is no basis in history or in any of the three philosophies or worldviews, and this society must seek its own basis.

This attempted fourth view may be seen as an 'inverted dualism', rejecting any objective sacred reality 'out there', and reducing the sacred, the spiritual and religion to a useful sets of values created by the secular culture itself.[8] These may still be called 'faiths' or 'scientific, modernized religions', but this is an abuse of language serving to mask the radicalness of what is happening. All is now secularized in the one single reality, in a mono-reality we call monism. The spirit world of the tribals is gone, the spiritual realm of the dualist faiths has been absorbed into this material world, and the Creator has been reduced to our own creativity. This is the philosophy of secularism.

Two new relations to the sacred

The first feature of the secular world is that there is no place here either for traditional forms of religion or for innovative movements that still serve the sacred and can be properly called 'religions'. It is hoped that the traditional mainline forms will die out, for they are still too established to attack directly. They may even be tamed, patronized, and retained for public ceremonial purposes. The new forms, however, are small, weak and without a long established following, so they can if possible be prevented from spreading and be driven out of existence now. We have surveyed some of the recent attempts at harassment and persecution, and how stubborn the response can be; but hopefully, this is a start on clearing the field for the secular society. It cannot tolerate independent religious vitality.

The second way of dealing with the sacred is to create an ersatz form that substitutes for the real thing, but keeps up the pretence of a relation between the secular and the sacred. Secular societies now are notable supporters of the new 'spirituality' that has become politically correct, and that claims to include the essence of the tribal or indigenous faiths as well as of the traditional religions in society's history. This challenges nobody, since it is 'made to measure' by a society for itself, and indeed by any individual wanting a comfortable spiritual sanction that is vague enough to avoid clash with anybody else's spirituality.

In this ersatz form of religion secular society affirms that everybody has a 'spiritual journey' that should be recorded and reflected upon as an affirmation of their own identity. This, however, reveals that 'spirituality' has no essential connection with religion; it refers to the distinctive capacity of human beings to transcend themselves by being self-conscious and self-critical, to transcend time by being imaginative about the past and the future, and to operate rationally.[9] Someone born and raised as an atheist in an atheist community may have as much spirituality as someone raised in a devout Quaker home. An individual's spiritual journey may run from the latter to the former, or vice versa. Joseph Vissarionovich, whose poor shoemaker father died early, was raised as her only surviving son by his deeply religious washerwoman mother who directed him towards the priesthood of the Georgian Orthodox Church. In 1899, just at the end of his seminary training, he was expelled since his 'spiritual journey' had branched away through the socialism of the day, and later led to the new name he gave himself in 1913,

Stalin (= Man of Steel), through the infighting among the Russian Marxists and finally towards the ruthless atheistic dictator and undisputed master of the USSR that he became. It was no less the spiritual journey of a well-educated and very intelligent man with substantial published works.

Spirituality therefore is a human quality which also has the capacity to subordinate one's self to that which transcends the human, to the divine or sacred. This is the religious relationship that may or may not develop in any explicit form, and in Stalin's case was repudiated.

In a secular society it is therefore quite safe and almost necessary in public life to identify with this nebulous, candy-floss 'religionless spirituality', without a history, doctrines or rituals. The doctrinal defect is met by New Age, Gaia, Earth Mother and primeval goddess beliefs,[10] or by imaginative, mystical versions of modern physics. The ritual defect is rapidly being remedied by dawn or hilltop ceremonies, libations, candles and fires, circle and other dances, and the techniques of the new spiritual therapies multiplying in Western societies. Indeed, there are now self-appointed ritual officiants who will oblige for a specialist's fee with a customized ritual for almost any occasion, in an attempt to sacralize it. This exposes the inner inadequacies of a secular culture, its structural vacuums, since rituals and ceremonies are essentially corporate traditions, not private inventions for a day.

In this dead-end way Western cultures are attempting to develop a fourth worldview. This seeks to replace the objective realities of the sacred in the historical tribal, dualist and duality views detailed above by a new subjective form of the sacred, our very own spirituality, rooted in ourselves in conjunction with our natural environment. As I have discussed elsewhere,[11] this leads to total pluralism, with consequent anarchy and the end of a culture.

Already, by the late 20th century, the failure of the Western attempt at a fourth worldview for a secular society has been revealed in the mounting list of insoluble social problems, which need not be detailed here; every daily newspaper and radio broadcast does it for us.

Many signs suggest that the sickness of Western culture may be terminal, and there are many prophets of doom to exploit them; but having been involved in the stubborn persistence of the religions in my own stories I have a quite different confidence for the future. I would apply the old adage that 'the blood of the martyrs is the seed of the church' to all the harassed and persecuted movements that have entered my stories. My analysis of why a secular society becomes so hostile to these new movements will also, I hope, offer them some encouragement. They will come to see themselves as part of a much larger story of a culture in trouble, indeed that they themselves are reflections of a troubled secular society's search for answers.

As a further comment, one cannot avoid the feeling that there is an element of wish-fulfilment in this secularism theory. May it not be a highly personal and widespread defence mechanism against the demands of all authentic religions within any of the three worldviews, rather than the next step in the historical process of working out once again the relation between the sacred and the secular? If this statement is resented and rejected as an *argumentum ad hominem*, then so be it; all positions come down to personal choice, to Polanyi's 'fiduciary stance', in the end.

It will be noted that I have said almost nothing about the third or duality worldview, which operates in terms of an absolute Creator and a semi-autonomous de-sacralized creation. Despite appearances this was not the actual practice of the Christendom experiment, and it took the rise of modern science to affirm such a creation and so to hasten the end of the false synthesis in Europe's mediaeval period. That this was an authentic and necessary Christian development is the thesis of my *The Roots of Science*. Now that science has finally thrown off the dualism that has haunted it since Descartes the way is clear for a new form of relation between the sacred and the secular, science being the chief organized representative of the latter. No one can foretell just what this will be, except that it will not be a revival of the Christendom mode. My *Frames of Mind: A Public Philosophy for Religion and Cultures* is an attempt to identify the framework for the new synthesis.

Further implications: within the churches

Besides the cultural considerations raised by our movements, they also apply to one of the current domestic issues within the churches themselves. This is whether the Christian Church is to be regarded as an 'inclusive' or an 'exclusive' body. The debate has arisen in the context of sexuality, and especially as to whether practising homosexuals may be included as members, and more especially as ordained ministers and leaders. This raises a basic question in the doctrine or theology of the Christian Church, that of defining the qualifications for membership and where the boundaries, if any, are to be drawn. In many denominations this is being bitterly debated, with pressure from the 'inclusivists' to open the traditional boundaries in this area to take in all who come within the love of God, which is boundless. The Church would then be primarily inclusive, with membership and leadership positions open to professed and practising homosexuals, and this position accepted without any discrimination as normal.

When we examine the five movements or bodies found in our stories it is clear that when they were harassed or persecuted they were being treated as excluded from the Church. The particular form this took for the Afrikaner Churches in South Africa was to suspend or terminate their membership in ecumenical bodies, in their case such as in the international Alliance of Reformed and Presbyterian Churches. It is also clear that however much I would fight for religious freedom on behalf of the Moonies or the Rastafari, I would on no account support their recognition as Christian bodies entitled to admission to Councils of Christian Churches. Although originally the Moonies were officially The Holy Spirit Association for the Unification of World Christianity, their applications for admissions to Council of Churches were always and correctly declined.

The Rastafari would never make such applications and I define them as a Christian derivative rather than a sect or cult; possibly the Unificationists should be seen in the same category, and also as in part as a Confucian and Taoist derivative. I have mentioned Scientology although I have not been involved personally to any extent; it might be difficult to call this even a Christian derivative, but it would certainly be excluded.

I have therefore been working with the exclusive category, and at other points also with the inclusive. I would defend the right of MRA members to any place in a Christian church, and some have in fact been bishops or prominent theologians. Despite their attitude for a period to apartheid the Afrikaner churches cannot be 'unchurched', and I came to be impressed by their theologically highly trained and orthodox ministry, the strength of their congregations and their maintenance of a Christian family life. I opposed their exclusion or boycotting in any form.

I have also had to decide how to regard the so-called African independent churches. These range over a wide spectrum, and I use a four-part typology ranging from what I call neo-primal movements (Christian elements modifying the tribal faiths), through synthetist (a mixture of both) to Hebraist (biblical but without a special place for Christ), and independent church (somehow within the always defective Christian category). Probably a majority intend to be Christian churches, however confusedly, and they would have to be examined individually.

When I applied the question 'Is this properly to be called a Christian Church?' to the Church of the Lord (Aladura) that I studied intensively, the only answer in that case had to be affirmative. It might be legalistic, and with a defective Christology, but it had to be included in the fourth group rather than in any of the others.

My stories have therefore raised the practical questions of inclusion and exclusion, and have given definite answers in each case. While these movements have not been involved with the current issue of homosexuality, the setting of boundaries and therefore of exclusion and inclusion has been important for them all. By the same token institutional church membership cannot be simply described by the single term 'inclusive'. At the same time it should be clear that this position does not limit one's personal relationships with the individuals or communities that are excluded, or make one less active in concern for their fair treatment by society. My own experience with bodies falling on either side of the boundary line should be sufficient testimony to this.[12] Some might go further and describe these stories as illustrating the life of a missionary on the margins and crossing the boundaries.

Further implications: from theology to ideology and back[13]

The last story, however, raises other questions again, since the Afrikaner churches were not minor bodies at the margins, nor new nor heretical, but orthodox bodies almost in the position of state churches in a culture then little affected by the inroads of secularism. The issue is how a theology can move into an ideology and then back again.

In 1857 the farmers in the large Dutch Reformed Church, decided to cease common worship with everyone on the farm, blacks and whites together. They began to set up separate worship for the two races, but it had almost nothing to do with apartheid, much less with Calvin of whom they had hardly ever heard. I have already noted that it was a pragmatic decision in the interests of the blacks themselves, giving them greater freedom and responsibility in their own churches with their own languages and making for more effective evangelism. It was not an ideology protecting the interests of the white class, but if anything just the reverse, an implicit biblical theology intended to further the welfare of the Black Africans.

From the late 19th century and into the 20th the DRC was dominated by an evangelical pietism, a-political, and largely derived from imported Scottish ministers who were not especially Calvinistic. It was the much smaller Reformed Church in Africa (the 'Doppers') which drew upon the late 19th century neo-Calvinist revival in Holland led by the great Abraham Kuyper, with his Free University of Amsterdam. The poet known as Totius (a pseudonym; 1877-1953) had been a young DRC chaplain in the Boer forces in the Anglo-Boer war and shared in this humiliation of his people. Then he went to the Free University of Amsterdam for his doctorate, and returned as a lonely would-be Calvinist but had to find a home in the much more Calvinstic Doppers, but with what we have seen to be a distorted Calvinist doctrine of election. We have also quoted Kuyper himself in his famous Stone Lectures on Calvinism at Princeton in 1895, declaring that the most advanced human races were those that were the most mixed, not the most racially pure – just the reverse of apartheid.

This bastardized Kuyperianism of Totius was then reinforced by a generation of graduate students who went to the German universities from the 1920s. After their recent treatment by the British the Boers/Afrikaners had naturally sympathized with Germany in World War I and avoided the universities of Britain and her allies after the war. In Germany they were prepared for the racial doctrines of the Nazis; Dr Verwoerd, whose daughter appears as hostess in my story, was one of these as a post-graduate student in 1926.

A third strand in the development of apartheid was the movement for the establishment of Afrikaans as the national language both spoken and written in place of Dutch. By 1919 Afrikaans had become the language of the DRC, and by 1925 was a recognized official language. Totius' father has been called the father of this movement, and his son played a large part in translating the Bible into Afrikaans by 1932. His highly emotional epic poems identified the sufferings and election of the Dutch settler people with those of biblical Israel; and we must remember that for long the Bible was the only book many Afrikaner families had. Through his poetry and his later position as professor of theology in the Doppers' university at Potchefstroom, he became a major influence in Afrikaner nationalism and the recovery of self-respect after the defeat in the war of 1899-1902.

Mainly from these three sources apartheid had become the ideology of the Afrikaner people, including their three churches. Although these had been caught up in the wider nationalist movement rather than led it, their theological basis had been virtually replaced by the new ideology. When in 1948 the Afrikaners won political power in South Africa, they went along with the radical implementation of separate development under Strijdom and Verwoerd, and in the eyes of the Western churches were to be banned and boycotted.

This critique was quite correct; ideology had replaced theology in the public life of these churches, and the sinister racial Broederbond had dominated its ministry. The Western adoption of a kind of apartheid in reverse by breaking off all relations with them was another matter, and here, as I have made plain in the story, I chose the opposite approach of bridge-building, with immense appreciation by my Afrikaner hosts. I also admired the impressive piety of their home life and the quality of the scholarship in their theological faculties – they probably had a better educated ministry than the majority of the Western churches that treated them as pariahs.

The theological faculties especially played a key part in the ultimate rejection of apartheid, particularly the heartland faculties in Stellenbosch[14] and Pretoria Universities. In Story Seven I have surveyed the early individual and joint theological protests; by 1982, 123 leading DRC ministers and theologians had sent an open letter to the General Synod declaring for reform, but the then moderator refused to accept it. I have told how by 1986, however, the Synod had elected a reforming moderator, the theologian Johan Heyns whose later murder I have reported, and how they had rejected apartheid, confessing the church's part in it. But the Western boycotters gave no support to those within the Afrikaner churches who fought this battle from within, often at great personal cost.

These churches have provided a clear model of how a church with a strong theological tradition and good facilities can nevertheless be carried along with great cultural and social changes and be used to provide an ideological justification for these changes – in this case to preserve the power and privileges of the whites. The more 'successful' a church has been in identifying with a people in their history and struggles and in serving them, the more difficulty it finds in standing over against new cultural developments hostile to its gospel and critiquing these, and the more it is liable to find its theological thinking distorted into an ideology that bolsters anti-Christian positions.

Although the original biblical and theological resources are suppressed or misused their potential remains intact, and in the end they burst through to critique and finally reject the ideology that has replaced them. All this, from theology to ideology and back again, happened in the Afrikaner churches within the short space of some five decades.

It is possible that the negative attitudes of Western churches may have prolonged rather than shortened this process. In any case most Western churches operate with a large unrecognized ideological element, which is no more than a rationalizing of their continuing denominational divisions or other practices, presented in theological dress. The clarity with which this happened in South Africa, as well as the remedy acting from within the permanent resources of the Christian faith, provide the wider meaning for my seventh story.

Epilogue

While these stories document the continuing harassment of religion in our own allegedly free Western societies, they also testify to a resilience and persistence that win through in the end. Thus MRA has had its Westminster Abbey semi-centennial celebration, some of the African independent churches now belong to Christian Councils and are almost feted by some ecumenists, the Rastafari in their homeland Jamaica are now an accepted part of the local scene, the Unification Church has won its freedom at least in Britain, and the Afrikaner Churches are restored to fellowship with the Christian world.

In other stories given only passing mention here and where such happy outcomes have not been possible, there has been public and sometimes official acknowledgement that the persecution was wrong – the Seventh Day Adventist mother, Lindy Chamberlain, at Ayer's Rock and the Davidians' debacle at Waco, Texas, are recent examples. The court decisions in favour of the Full Gospel Mission and the Exclusive Brethren in New Zealand against the government and the media show further victories for religious freedom.

In quite a different context, in August 2000 the New Zealand Court of Appeal quashed a ban on the distribution of two videos containing a Christian criticism of homosexuality that had been imposed by the Film and Literature Board of Review, and subsequently upheld by the High Court. The videos had been granted restricted viewing in 1994 and under constant pressure from the pro-homosexuality Human Rights Action Group the restriction had been increased in 1996 and become a total ban in 1997. The Appeal court was emphatic on the priority of freedom of expression enshrined in the Bill of Rights over other legislation concerned with discrimination against classes of people or censorship of objectionable material. I am in no doubt that the original banning was an attempt to suppress a Christian viewpoint by an agency of the secular state with members already committed to non-Christian positions. Once again, it was the courts which stood for religious freedom in this country, but only after a six-year determined effort by those denied that freedom.

While we are told that 'life, liberty and the pursuit of happiness' are among our 'inalienable rights',[15] we are also reminded that 'The condition upon which God has given liberty to man is eternal vigilance'.[16] This is especially true for religious liberty in a secular society, where attacks on religions may appear suddenly, sparked by the smallest incident and lacking any apparent rationale. My prediction is that harassment and attacks will increase along with a more secularized public arena, but will focus less on the marginal or newer faiths and more on the Christian religion in particular. The great Asian faiths will be protected meanwhile by their association with the non-white races, so that opponents would be accused of racism, that most politically incorrect of sins. The major Christian festivals are already under fire, while no one dare attack the festivals of the other faiths. There is no basis in history or experience for relaxing 'eternal vigilance' on behalf of religious freedom.

This is the first and most obvious thing these stories say to us. Since religion lies at the heart of human existence and of all cultures they also offer radical comment on modern Western secular cultures and their concocted spiritualities. My stories therefore combine to offer a case study of this aspect of our own culture, and so serve the purposes of the DeepSight Trust, as 'a New Zealand initiative for religion and cultures' that is likewise necessary in every part of the Western world.

If this larger cultural concern is beyond the reach of some of us then these stories may serve to illumine our own humbler personal stories by helping us to reflect upon the route taken by our individual journeys. Few will, I expect, fail to join me in finding unexpected diversions or new paths that were not visible on the map when we began, or small events along the way that have later proved of great significance in our lives. I have shared some of these features in my own journey, and given my own theological interpretation of them in terms of a kindly Providence that could laugh at my journey plans in the light of what lay ahead, all unknown to me. Perhaps in the end, when I find that Providence has always had the last laugh, I may find myself joining in by laughing at myself and at the plans that never worked out – thank God!

Not everyone may share my interpretation or agree with the title of this book, but I suspect most will resonate somewhere with its contents and experiences, and find some amusement as they reflect upon the gains or losses in the might-have-beens of their own affairs.

Endnotes

Introduction

1   While writing these lines, I came across Stephen Pattison's *The Faith of the Managers: When Management becomes Religion*, London: Cassell, 1997. He has been both theologian and in public management, and offers a unique critique of the management revolution. He points out the devastating failures of attempts at complete central planning in the older nations of Europe and Asia and the newer ones in Africa, with their five- and ten-year plans, and the similar failures in the management society to plan fulfilment of the 'mission' embodying the 'vision' which every corporate body is expected to have. And who planned for the collapse of the Berlin Wall or the advent of the AIDS pandemic? Pattison well knows the value of plans on a modest scale, but otherwise neither life nor history run 'according to plan'. My stories add illustrations to his theme.

Story One

1   He continues to write, including (with his late wife Honor) the song 'For Australia' that was sung at the Bicentennial celebrations in the Sydney Opera House, and at the opening of the new Parliament House in Canberra in 1988. In 1993 he published *The Honeyman and Other Poems*.

2   Garth Lean, *The Life of Frank Buchman*, London 1985, and in the USA as *On the Tail of a Comet: a Life of Frank Buchman*, Helmers & Howard, 1988.

3   On this see my *Frames of Mind. A Public Philosophy for Religion and Cultures*, Auckland: The DeepSightTrust, 2001.

Story Two

1   This research issued in the two volumes published by the Clarendon Press, Oxford in

1967 as *African Independent Church*. I am told they remain the most detailed study of any church in Africa. One could tell many more illuminating stories from the close involvement I had with this church over some eight years in West Africa and in other senses ever since.

2   See my 'Monogamy a mark of the Church?', *International Review of Missions*, no. 219, vol. 55, 1966, pp. 313-21.

3   Our persecution theme was illustrated in reverse, as it were, when there was a meeting of local colonial administrators to consider suppressing Oshitelu's movement, but decided against this after being reminded by the legal officer that it was always rather tricky for governments to attempt to deal with prophets.

4   I have been privileged to visit such movements in many parts of the world, even if only for a day, and they all have interesting stories, fortunately mostly without severe persecution. I shall list some examples here to give the feel of the variety and distribution. In Africa, the God's Kingdom Society in Calabar in eastern Nigeria, where during worship the founder sat in shorts humbly on the floor; in southern Malawi, The Providence Industrial Mission clearly named from a Western source, whose founder died in revolt against the colonial authority; and the amaNazaretha or Nazarene Baptist Church among the Zulu, whose founder, Isaiah Shembe, turned African culture upside down by publicly washing the feet of his disciples at his holy city of Ekuphakameni. This church features beautifully in the 'Zulu Zion' instalment of the BBC TV series on religions, *The Long Search*. In Jamaica there was the remnant of the Bedwardites who had led to martial law a century ago; before Bedward's aged granddaughter I tried to tell them something of their opposite numbers in the African independents by demonstrating how these danced in church. In North America there were independent churches where I was able to preach or speak in Florida, Oklahoma, and especially on the Hopi Indian Reservation in Arizona, where traditional Hopi religion also is still alive and well. In the Philippines it was the Iglesia ni Cristo (Church of Christ) with its beautiful churches, and the Philippine Independent Church at whose joint seminary with the Philippine Episcopal Church (mainline) I stayed. In Fiji there was the day up the Rewa River delta visiting villages of the self-reliant Daku community founded by prophet Ratu Emosi on reclaimed ground half a century ago. Then over in New Britain there was the visit to the 'Egg Prophet' village (founded 1950s) of Melki, with his fear of persecution by the aggressive coastal Tolai who had driven the meeker Baining up into the hills – shown by the hopefully protective Australian flag still being flown from the sacred ground years after independence. While some of these could tell of severe persecutions, I was not personally involved as in the stories I have told.

5   See my 'Prophets and Politics: a Nigerian test case', *Bulletin of the Society for African Church History*, 2(1), 1965, pp. 97-118; reprinted in my *Religious Innovation in Africa*, Boston: G.K. Hall, 1979, pp. 133-145.

6   A further scholarly study of Rua 66 years after the events, is Judith Binney, 'Maunga-pohatu Revisited: or, How a Government underdeveloped a Maori Community', *Journal of the Polynesian Society*, 92(3), 1983, pp. 352-92; good road access to this once 'New Jerusalem' has recently been again denied. See also the next chapter, on the trials connected with the Rastafari. On the positive contribution of these movements to development see my 'African independent churches and economic development', *World Development*. 8(7-8), June-July 1980, pp. 523-33; repr. in K.P. Jameson and C.K. Wilbur (eds.), *Religious Values and Development*, Oxford: Pergamon Press 1981, pp. 523-33.

7   These unhappy stories were the burden of the Burns Lectures given in the University
     of Otago in 1976; a full annotated bibliography will be found in the New Zealand and
     other sections of *Oceania*, being vol. 3 of the set referred to in the note at the end of
     the introduction.

8   When teaching religious studies in the new University of Nigeria in the mid-1960s we
     had as a student the first member of an independent church, the Christ Apostolic
     Church, to go to university. I was his 'personal tutor' so when he returned for a second
     year with nothing more than one shilling for the year, he came in his distress to me. He
     was a very good student, so I had no option but to break my rule of never having
     money dealings with students, and I offered to pay his first term's fees. I had recently
     been the guest of a well-to-do church in New Jersey. So I wrote to this church, told
     them the story, and their Men's Fellowship offered his fees for the next term. They
     then continued this support right through to post-graduate study in Montreal, and he
     was able to visit them to thank them. Now he is a respected senior lecturer in religious
     studies in a Nigerian university, and a leader in his original church.

Story Three

1   For a scholarly, detailed account of this development together with the special appeal
     of the Psalter to the Rastafari, see N.S. Murrell, 'Tuning Hebrew Psalms to Reggae
     rhythms: Rastas' revolutionary lamentations for social change', *Cross Currents* 50(4),
     Winter 2000-01, 12pp.

2   That this rehabilitation was not confined to Campbell is indicated by the testimony in
     court of one of his associates that: "A Rasta is a peaceful man. You don't go looking
     for fights. He goes to try to settle the matter in another way." This brings the East
     Coast members closer to those in Auckland.

3   The police were in fact contacted a number of times; at some stage Donnelly spoke to
     Detective Hikawai and told him "to come on up", and passing motorists who saw the
     scene phoned the police and 111.

4   Joseph Owens S.J., *Dread: The Rastafarians of Jamaica*, 1976 in Kingston: Sangster's
     Book Stores; repr. London: Heinemann Educational Books, 1979. The foundation
     study remains M.G. Smith et al, *The Rastafarian Movement in Kingston, Jamaica*,
     London: Jamaican High Commission 1960 (and many reprints), a Government report
     marking the turning point in public attitudes. In 1992 my bibliography on the movement
     contained 343 items – see *Bibliography of New Religious Movements in Primal
     Societies. Vol.6, Caribbean*, Boston: G.K. Hall. Now, with Reggae music also included
     published items have mushroomed, as the Internet bears witness. The best recent
     overview is in a collection of essays edited by Daniel S. Murray et al, *Chanting Down
     Babylon*, Philadelphia University Press 1998.
     The best and most up-to-date theological evaluation is probably W.D. Spencer's *Dread
     Jesus*, London: S.P.C.K. 1999. He surveys the various minority forms of Rastafarianism,
     with different beliefs ranging from 'Selassie as God' to 'the God of Selassie'. The
     latter could give rise to a 'Selassian Christian Church' in a sense similar to that of the
     Lutheran (Christian) Church. For extended review, see M. Introvigne on *Dread Jesus*
     at the website: www.cesnur.org
     I have not heard of what the Rastafari have made of the subsequent history of their
     African Messiah. He ruled for 44 years, until overthrown and probably murdered in
     1975 aged 83 by the new Marxist regime, which fell in 1991. In November 2000 his
     remains were reinterred beside those of his wife in the Holy Trinity Cathedral in Addis

Ababa. The current government remains highly critical of him, and press reports made no mention of any Rastafarian presence.

Story Four

1   Subsequently published in the Proceedings as 'The new religions as free partners in a plural society', in H.O. Thompson (ed.), *Global Outreach: Global Congress of the World Religions*, Barrytown: Unification Theological Seminary 1987, pp. 215-25.

2   Published as: 'The relationship between development and new religious movements in the tribal societies of the Third World', in F. Ferre and R.H. Mataragnon (eds.) *God and Global Justice: Religion and Poverty in an Unequal World.* New York; Paragon House Press 1985, pp. 84-110; repr. as 'Tradition and Change in Africa', in *The World and I* . Washington D.C.: 1(1), Jan. 1986, pp. 246-61, without footnotes.

3   Books by ex-members have titles such as: I was a Watch Tower Slave/Convent Prisoner, etc., but in fairness I must mention a book in this genre that belies its title: *Heavenly Deception*, by Chris Elkins, Eastbourne: Kingsway Publications 1982. It is especially valuable for (1) His parents' counter-productive attempts at de-programming; (2) Nevertheless his efforts to maintain family contact; (3) How easily he left the Moonies; (4) His respect for the positive experiences while a member; (5) The unpleasant first-hand accounts of Moon; (6) His subsequent efforts to replace their version of 'love' with his new Christian love for them. All these features, at least for this one member, contradict the popular image.

4   George D. Chryssides, *The Advent of Sun Myung Moon, The Origins, Beliefs and Practices of the Unification Church*, London: Macmillan, 1991, ch.7, discusses 'The Blessing' including the Holy Wine and marriage ceremonies. This is also perhaps the best general sympathetic but critical academic account of this Church.

5   I owe most of the update information to an excellent paper by Massimo Introvigne, Director of the Centre for Studies on New Religions, in Turin: 'From the Unification Church to the Unification Movement, 1994-1999: Five years of Dramatic Changes.' This and much other reliable information is available on their website: www.cesnur.org

6   Many organizations seem interested in this area, known as the Pantanal. See the website: www.pantanal.org – and note the absence of reference to the Unification Church.

Story Five

1   The King's College Centre for new religious movements concentrated on the current 'sects and cults', and was actually developed by a young lecturer, Peter Clarke, from the early 1980s. Although when on visits to King's College I enquired about this I was never shown anything; in Birmingham I was able to show Professor Sutherland three rooms of resources and three staff. Now under Professor Clarke the Centre must have grown and the fine *Journal of Contemporary Religion* emanates from King's. Professor Sutherland's distinguished career began as Chief Inspector of Schools in England. His meteoric rise attests great administrative abilities, as well as being always on the right side, including that of the Attorney-General in the Unification Church charges. This was the one time when officialdom let him down, and he was defeated by one of his 'sects and cults', even though he knew excusably little of the Moonies, and inexcusably less of the meaning of the term 'Christian', when he charged the defendants with wrongly and knowingly adopting this term. The new Attorney-General fortunately saved Professor Sutherland from exposure in the witness box. The whole incident

reveals the difficult of evaluating 'experts', especially in the field of religion, and when someone concerned has been chief editor of a massive volume, *The World's Religions*, London: Routledge 1988, to which I contributed the section 'New Religious Movements: Africa'.

Story Six

1   Richard Crossman, *The Diaries of a Cabinet Minister*. London: H. Hamilton; and J. Cape, vol. 3, 1981, especially pp. 134, 176, 276-7, 294, 319.

2   The attorney has reported every twist and turning in this case in a long report in Russian in the *Independent Psychiatric Journal*. All this and the unexpected outcome are available from the website of the Centre for Studies on New Religions in Turin, CESNUR: www.cesnur.org   There is also a report of a similar legal victory on 13 September 2000 for the Unificationists in Germany. It never stops.

3   This case has been well studied by James T. Richardson in 'Public opinion and the Tax Evasion Trial of Reverend Moon', *Behavorial Sciences and the Law*, 10, 1992, pp. 53-63.

4   It is in France, the very home of the Enlightenment, and with a Revolution to establish human rights, that the most atrocious persecutions of the Unification Church and many other new bodies have occurred at State level. CESNUR above keeps up to date files on these and other European developments not reported in the media. James T. Robinson gives a good summary of European legal and government institutions dithering over new religious movements, with consequent injustices, in 'Minority religions ("Cults") and the law: comparisons of the United States, Europe and Australia', *University of Queensland Law Journal*, 18(2), 1995, pp. 194-6; also more fully in 'New religions and religious freedom in Eastern and Central Europe', in I. Borowik and G. Babinski (eds.), *New Religious Phenomena in Central and Eastern Europe*, Krakow, 1997, pp. 257-282. In the rest of the world the major clash seems to be the attempted suppression of the massive Chinese religious movement Falun Gong. China has a long history of similar developments, including the semi-Christian Taiping revolutionary movement in the mid-19th century that cost some 30 million lives. My bibliography of European language materials on Taiping is about to be published by Yale University Divinity School. There is masses of material on Falun Gong on the Internet in reference to these two words – especially 'Falun Gong 101' by M. Introvigne.

Story Seven

1   I shall deal with the development of the apartheid ideology more fully in the next chapter.

2   I never learned of the outcome; whether anyone was ever charged with this cold-blooded murder.

Eight

1   See Dean M. Kelley, 'A massacre and its aftermath', *First Things*, no. 53, May 1995, pp. 22-37. There is now a large literature on this government atrocity.

2   In 1995 five of the seven judges on the High Court were raised as Catholics.

3   For a survey of the unsatisfactory Australian government relations to religious freedom, with case studies of minorities and new religions summarized, see James T. Richardson, 'Minority religions ("Cults") and the Law: comparisons of the United States, Europe and Australia', *University of Queensland Law Journal*, 18(2), 1995, pp. 183-207, especially from p. 196. Professor Richardson has written widely on this subject.

4   Full account in Romilly Fraser's *The God Squad*, Auckland 1978.

5   I rely on correspondence with the Brethren and Dr. Smith, and on the transcripts of the judgments of the High Court judge and the three Appeal Court judges, as well as press reports.

6   For the persistence of religion see my *Frames of Mind*, ch.1

7   I am quite aware that some movements engage in totally unacceptable practices; but this is not a new phenomenon and should be dealt with under existing or amended laws that cover such things as polygamy (legally banned for the Mormons long ago), human sacrifice or restraint, and matters covered by health or child protection regulations.

8   It is not unfair to observe that this is essentially the position of Professor Lloyd Geering, presented with skill, clarity, and much acceptance by the media for several decades. That it matches the culture I am describing is dramatically demonstrated by the New Zealand New Year honours list for the year 2001. Here, in addition to his earlier CBE, he is the only one awarded the top honour (apart from the limited Order of Merit itself) of Principal Companion of the New Zealand Order of Merit. Possibly nowhere else than New Zealand could the issues be set forth publicly in this way. For Professor Geering himself, of course, this is a great and hard-earned achievement.

9   I have explored the nature of spirituality in my 'The human and the spiritual', in *Selly Oak Journal* (Birmingham), no. 8, Spring 1988, pp. 16-23.

10   It is unfortunate that the authentic movement for the liberation of women in Western societies has been confused with an ideology that revels in the varieties of spirituality, promoting women's power, almost like a Marxian class. Women's magazines regularly illustrate this concern with spirituality.

11   See chs. 10-11 of *The Roots of Science*, and the gatefold diagram at the rear.

12   I am grateful to my then minister, Dr Graham Redding, for drawing my attention to these ecclesiastical issues after I had told these stories at evening services in our church.

13   Much of the following material appeared in briefer form in the 'Face to Faith' column of *The Guardian* newspaper in Britain, 22 June 1987, p. 22. There is also some degree of repetition with Story Seven.

14   Verwoerd had been appointed a professor of applied psychology at Stellenbosch in 1927.

15   The American Declaration of Independence, 1776.

16   John P. Curran, *Speech on the Right of Election of the Lord Mayor of Dublin*, 1790.

Aberdeen (and Moonies) 69f.
Aberdeen University 71.
Adejobi, Adeleke 30ff., 33, 36, 45, 47.
Afrikaans language 145.
Afrikaner Churches Story Seven, *passim*.
Afrikaner missions 120f.
Alcoholics Anonymous 24.
Alton, David, M.P. 110.
Amnesty International 110f.
ancestors 40.
Anglican vicar (Birmingham) 74.
Anglo-Boer War 117.
apartheid 118f., 124, 127, 128.
arson (Ruatoria area) 62.
Attorney-General (U.K.) 92-95; initiates
  charges 92; withdraws charges 94f.;
  costs against 95.
Auckland Grammar School 14.
Australian volunteers 72.
autobiography 132f.

Babylon (for Rastafari) 118.

Baillie, John (Prof.) 23, 28.
Barker, Eileen (Dr.) 87, 89, 93.
Barth, Karl (and apartheid) 119, 121.
Bates, J.M. 19.
Bedward, Alexander (prophet) 51.
Bevan, Aneurin, M.P. 100.
Bible 59, 61, 68, 118, 124, 145.
Bible Training Institute (Auckland) 3.
Bible Training Institute (Glasgow) 45.
Biko, Steve 125.
Birmingham University 45f., 130.
Black, W. Bower (Rev.) 15, 22.
Bosch, Annemie 126, 128.
Bosch, David (Professor) 126, 128.
Boshoff, Carel (Professor) 120, 127.
Botha, P.W. (President) 128.
boycotting 128, 129, 146.
Braid, Garrick (prophet) 42f.
brainwashing 68, 79, 88.
Branch Davidian *see* Davidian.
British Council 115.
British Council of Churches 107, 108,

109, 128.
Broederbond (Afrikaners) 117f., 121ff.
Brunner, Emil 21.
Buchan, John 16.
Buchman, Frank 20, 28.

Calvin, John (and apartheid) 118f.
Campbell, Christopher 56 *et seq.*; 1986
　trial transcript 63f.
Catherwood, Fred (Sir, MEP) 109.
Caux (MRA centre) 27, 28.
Centre for Studies of New Religions,
　Turin 103 n2; 111 n4.
Chamberlain, Lindy (Ayer's Rock) 135.
Charity Commissioners (U.K.) 91f.
Cherubim and Seraphim 41, 53.
Christendom 138f.
Christology 38.
Church definitions as exclusive/inclusive
　142ff.
Church of Scotland 23, 26, 28, 71, 85,
　86.
Church of the Lord (Aladura) Story Two,
　passim.
Clark, (Dr.) (psychiatrist) 87f.
Collie, John (Prof.) 22.
colonialism, South Africa 117f.
Coloureds (South Africa) 116.
concentration camps (for Boers) 117.
Cottrell Report 106-9.
Cottrell, Richard, MEP 105-8.
Council of Ministers (European) 109.
Court of Appeal, (N.Z.) 147f.
Cracknell, Kenneth (Rev.) 96.
Crossman, Richard, M.P. 100f.

D.D. (Melbourne Coll. Div.) 34.
Daily Mail libel case 88-91.
dancing, in worship 32, 46.
Davidian Community, Texas 135.
Day of the Covenant (Afrikaner) 117.
Dennning (Lord) 95.
Depression, 1930s 13.

divination 40.
Donnelly, Luke 57 *et seq.*; killing of
　Campbell 60ff; Armed Offenders'
　Squad 57f.; as Parliamentary candidate
　63; transcript of the trial 63f.
"Doppers" *see* Reformed Church of
　Africa
dreams, as revelation 46.
Driberg, Tom, MP 100.
drug addict 70f.
Dunbar (Unification Church introduction
　centre) 69.
Durham University 17, 25.
Dutch East Indies Company 106.
Dutch Reformed Church Story Seven,
　passim.
Dyer, Hensley 54, 56.

Enlightenment, The 111-12.
European constitutions 111.
European Parliament 105 *et seq.*
Exclusive Brethren in Britain 103; in
　New Zealand 136.

Falun Gong movement (China) 11 n4.
Ferguson, John 73ff.
Forster, Norvela, MEP 106.
Foster Report (on Scientology) 101.
Fourah Bay College 17.
Fox, Tom 62.
Full Gospel Mission (N.Z.) 98, 147.

Garvey, Marcus 49.
Germany (and Afrikaners) 119.
Geyer, John (Rev.) 51ff.
Ghana 39, 43f., 56.
Goldsmiths College 16.
Great Trek (South Africa) 117.

Haile Selassie 49f., 54, 59, 66.
Handsworth (Birmingham) 52.
Hare Krishna in Britain 102.
Harvard University 87f.

Hastings (N.Z.) 13, 20.
healing 39f.
Herron, David (Rev.) 14, 21.
Heyns, Johan (Professor) 124f.
Hikawai (Detective) 59.
Hikurangi, Mount 58f.
Holy Wine ceremony (marriage) 81.
homosexuality 143, 148.
Huddleston, Trevor (Archbishop) 129.
human rights 111-13; sanctions for 112.

ideology 144-7; sources of 145.
influenza epidemic, 1918 13, 41.

Jamaica 48, 51, 54, 65.
Jones, R.V. (Professor) 96.
Jonestown, Guyana 76.

Kelly, Dean (Rev.) 94.
kidnapping (by families) 76.
Kimbangu, Simon (prophet) 42.
Kimbanguism 39.
Klerk, F.W. de (President) 128.
Korea   see Unification Church.
Krylova, Galina A. (lawyer) 103.
Kuypers, Abraham 145.

"love-bombing" (Unificationists) 70.

magic 40.
Mahi Tahi Foundation (N. Z.) 53f., 63.
Mahuika, Api 59, 63.
Mamelodi, Pretoria 123.
management, of churches 12 n1.
Mandela, Nelson 44, 128f.
Mangaroa Prison 58.
marijuana 56ff.
Marley, Bob 54.
Meiring, Piet (Rev.) 125.
Mennonites 33ff.
Menzies, Ivan 21.
messianism 66, 68.
Michener, J.A. (*The Covenant*) 116.

Moon, Sun Myung Story Four *passim*.
"Moonies" Story Four *passim*; employing 72; study with 74, 75; defending 79f.
Moral Rearmament (MRA) 18; Story One *passim*; British parliament and, 100; critique of 27ff.
Mormons in U.K. 99f.
Mowat, Robin 25.

names, of churches 39.
Napier (N.Z.) 13.
Naudé, Beyers 124.
"necklacing" 123.
New Age 141.
New College, Edinburgh 22.
new religious movements 9, 38f.; world distribution 42 n4.
Nkrumah (President) 43.

Ohope marae 64.
Old Testament 17.
Oosthuizen, G.C. (Professor) 115, 131.
Opoho, Dunedin 11, 16.
Oshitelu, Josiah 36f., 41.
Oxford Groups 20.

parents (of sect or cult members) 73, 76, 78.
Parihaka 136.
Paton, Alan 124.
Pauw, Berthold (anthropologist) 131.
Peoples Community Radio Line 52.
Perry, Norman (Sir) 42, 53f., 58, 61, 63.
persecution, religious Stories Five and Six *passim*; 20th c. 84f.; in U.S.A. 103f., 135; in Australia 97f.; in New Zealand 98; in Western world, 133f., 137; in non-Western world 133f.; video banning (N.Z.) 148; increase projected 148.
Ph.D. research 25, 33.
philosophy, studying 15.
Polanyi, Michael 142.

police (South Africa) 125.
polygamy 36, 38.
Porteous, Will (Dr.) 21.
Press Council (U.K.) 89.
Pretorius, Hennie (Dr.) 131.
privacy acts 109.
Psalms, among Rastafari 51, 66.

Ras Tafari 49.
Rastafari Story Three *passim*; abroad 65;
  as religious movement 65f.
Ratana Church 41, 53.
"reasonings" (Rastafarian) 66.
Reformed Church in Africa ('Doppers')
  145.
reggae music 54, 55.
religious freedom 111; *et passim*.
Ringatu religion 43, 53, 136.
ritual officiants 141.
Rua (prophet) 38, 43, 58, 62, 88, 136.
Ruatoria 56, 57, 62, 63.
Russian persecution of Moonies 103.
Ryburn, Hubert (Rev.) 21.

Salvation Army 85, 137.
Schumann, Robert 28.
Scientologists in Britain 100f.; in Italy
  102; in New Zealand 101, 143.
Scottish Episcopal Church 87.
"sects and cults" 68.
secularism 140ff.
secularism worldview for 139f.; failure
  of 141.
Selly Oak Colleges 42, 45, 72ff., 129.
Seventh Day Adventists 9, 135.
Shenk, Wilbert R. 35.
Sheshamane (Ethiopia) 49, 56.
Sierra Leone 17, 30.
Simmonds, Richard, M.E.P. 106.
slavery, in Jamaica 48.
Smart, Ninian (Professor) 89, 93.
Smith, Nick, M.P. (Dr.) 136.
Smith, Nico (Professor) 119-23.

sociology of religion 137f.
South Africa, unique history 116f.
spirit world (Unificationists) 82f.
spirituality 140f.
squatter camp, Capetown 122.
Stalin, Joseph 140f.
Stellenbosch University 121f., 146.
Strijdom, J.L. 127.
Sun Myung Moon Story Four *passim*;
  defending 80; own family 83; South
  American plans 82; tax evasion charge
  80, 103-5; visa problems 79f., 96f.
Sutherland, Stewart (Professor, Sir) 94.
Swaziland 44.

T.V. programmes 74; Independent TV
  87f., 124.
Tanczos, Nandor (M.P.) 64, 65.
Te Kooti (Ringatu founder) 43, 58, 136.
The Press (Christchurch, N.Z.) 136.
The Washington Times 78.
Thompson, Jack 73.
Thompson, Raymond, trial of 62.
Thornton-Duesbury, J.P. 25.
Thrower, James (Dr.) 138.
Thwaites, Michael 23.
Torrance, Iain (Rev.) 86, 89f.
Totius (Afrikaner poet, etc.) 145.
Treurnicht, André (Dr.) 126.
tribal/transtribal 40, 65.
Tutu, Desmond (Bishop) 128f.
Twelve Tribes of Israel 52, 55, 56.

Unification Church Story Four *passim*;
  Divine Principle 68; economic base 68;
  arranged marriages 73; changes in 81f.;
  community good works 72, 85f.;
  conferences 75, 76f.; ex-members 78f.,
  82; finance 77f.; 'front' organizations
  80; in New Zealand 78f.; marriage
  blessings 80f.; pedlar's licence 85;
  recent teachings 82f.; secret teaching
  93; University of Bridgeport 82; U.S.

seminary 76.
United Church in Nigeria 46.
University de la Plata 97.
University of Parma, Seminar 111-13.

Vervoerd, H.F. (President) 121, 127.
visas, denial of 79f.
Visser't Hooft, W.A. 22, 35.

Waitai, Rana (Superintendent) 59.
Walls, Andrew (Professor) 12, 34f., 72.

Watson, Alan (Rev.) 15, 19, 20, 22.
Weaver, Edwin 34f.
Wilson, Bryan (Dr.) 92.
women, place of 41, 65.
World Council of Churches 36, 42, 45.
worldviews, 3 possible 138f.

Zion Christian Church 44.
Zion City Moriah 44.
Zionists 39, 114, 131.
Zyl, Danie van 131.